From
Contact to
Contract

Dianna Booher

Dearborn™
Trade Publishing
A **Kaplan Professional** Company

Vice President and Publisher: Cynthia A. Zigmund
Acquisitions Editor: Michael Cunningham
Senior Project Editor: Trey Thoelcke
Interior Design: Lucy Jenkins
Cover Design: Design Solutions
Typesetting: the dotted i

Published by Dearborn Trade Publishing, a Kaplan Professional Company

Printed in the United States of America

03 04 05   10 9 8 7 6 5 4 3 2 1

Library of Congress Cataloging-in-Publication Data

Booher, Dianna Daniels.
    From contact to contract : 496 proven sales tips to generate more leads, close more deals, exceed your goals, and make more money / Dianna Booher.
        p.   cm.
    Includes index.
    ISBN 0-7931-6800-7
    1. Selling.   I. Title.
    HF5438.25.B6543 2003
    658.85—dc21

                                                            2003009721

C o n t e n t s

YOU CAN GET THERE FROM HERE . . .

Stepping off the plane and headed toward Baggage Claim, Grant noticed the limo driver to his left holding the sign "Thompson." The driver took his bag and Grant followed him. So this is how it felt to get the celebrity treatment. Much better than the typical reception—fly in, hustle for a taxi, or grab a tram to the rental car lot.

If this was the kind of treatment they gave the *nominees* for Sales Professional of the Year, what could he expect if he won? Flying the top 2 percent to Hawaii for the week. Not bad. And if he won tonight? What then? Grant leaned back on the soft leather seat, poured himself a drink, opened the newspaper, and settled in as the driver walked around to the driver's side and climbed in.

He skimmed the headlines and then flipped on his cell phone. "Val?"

"Are you there yet?" she asked.

"Almost. I'm on the way to the hotel. Where are you?"

"Just landed. How did the interview go? When's the article coming out? What kind of things did they ask you? Did you get to tell them about how your helicopter was what saved that entire family during the evacuation after the tornado? I can't wait until the article runs. Are you the only one they interviewed for the story?"

"Do I get a choice of which of those I answer?" Grant teased. "Or should I just start in the middle and work my way out?"

"In the middle."

"Fine. April. How the helicopters worked. No."

"How can you do that?"

"If you can ask 'em, I can answer 'em."

"Gotta hang up and grab my bag."

"Okay. See you when you get here."

Grant slipped the cell phone back into his jacket and checked his watch. If she didn't miss her second flight, Val would be joining him in four more hours. Herself a seasoned sales rep for a software company, she knew how to cut through the typical airline spiel to get the real truth about whether they were or weren't going to take off. She'll be here. He nodded to himself again for reassurance. She'll be here.

Grant opened his briefcase, pulled out the tiny square box inside, and cracked the lid ever so slightly. Still there. Val had no idea he planned to ask the big question. His biggest "close" yet, although he'd tried a few trial closes along the way. He'd thought long and hard about taking this step after seeing Cinda struggle for two long years with cancer before she died. But once he'd decided to make the commitment, he couldn't get it done fast enough.

His thoughts floated to the article that soon would be running in his industry's largest journal, featuring his quotes and his product—that should generate even more leads. What a coup that had been! The press had picked up the story of the dramatic rescue where his plane had transported an injured family of tornado victims to the hospital in time to save their lives.

His cell phone rang. "Hello."

"Grant, this is Josh Frazier. Have you got a minute?"

"Sure. What can I help you with?"

"Well, after you left that proposal with me last week for the new helicopter at Westin for the police department, I thought it was a done deal. Thought we were just going to take it before city council, take a vote, and voilà, we'd have the helicopter. But nothing's that simple, right? Now, it looks like it's going to cost me my job."

"What do you mean?" Grant asked. He had grown particularly fond of this prospect during the long sales cycle as he'd worked with the city officials to educate them about his plane and the accompanying training their pilots needed to fly in emergency situations. In fact, the article that Val had been so excited about highlighted the lives saved because of the new design of their planes.

Grant couldn't imagine selling any other product—one that he didn't think really made a difference in how people did their work or lived their lives. He'd been a fighter pilot "in his other life," as he always put it, before finally ending up selling planes to city governments and hospitals. Grant had appreciated his product from the user perspective long before he had signed on to sell it. Passion—that's what he felt. Passion about planes, and Val.

Grant ended the conversation with Josh, giving him some pointers on how to shepherd the proposal around the pitfalls of city politics.

This was another part of the job that he loved—helping his clients, like Josh Frazier, do theirs. Though technically competent, Josh had the personality of a duffle bag. With such customers, Grant had to micromanage their manners and their mouth. But he didn't mind. That's what sales professionals do—practice a little psychology on the side.

The limo driver pulled into the hotel and let him out. When Grant gave them his name at the registration desk, he discovered that someone had already checked him in. A nice fruit basket was waiting inside the room. "Congratulations on being at the top of the bunch" was written on the card stuck to the bananas.

Grant looked at his watch. Just enough time to make a few calls and take a short nap before dressing for the big opening event. The last voicemail was the one he'd been waiting for: "You got the contract. The hospital executives signed off on three planes."

Grant jumped off the bed. "Yes!" He started to dial Val, but remembered she'd be on her second leg of the flight. Okay, calm down, he advised himself as he plopped back down on the bed. Everyone would know soon enough.

Awards. Featured in the press. A hero for your clients. Products you feel passionate about. How do you get to this stage in your own career?

Grant started with the basics and never let up. Even today, Grant continues to market himself, still prospects every day, consults with his clients for the best solution, negotiates winning outcomes, updates his skills and strategies regularly, and latches on to innovative ideas daily.

The tips and guidelines presented in this book will help you do the same. The tips will take you through the complete sales cycle: Chapter 1 provides help in researching and profiling your perfect prospect. Tips include how to cut through the clutter and screeners—to introduce yourself with credibility—without wasting your prospect's time or your own. The tips in Chapter 2 deal with conducting the consultative conversation: how you structure your sales conversation, how you listen, what you say, how you phrase it.

Chapter 3 leads you through a formal presentation of your product or service—the do's and don'ts of presenting persuasively rather than walking into the client's office and "winging it." One of the worst ways to deliver a sales proposal—and one of the most common—is to hand the document to a prospect and say, "Let's just walk through this together." Tips in this chapter will give you options for a high-impact presentation.

Chapter 4 offers help in gaining commitment from your clients and leading them through implementation. Far too many prospects "commit" to buy, but fail to take the next steps that actually close the sale and bring in the commissions and client results. Tips in Chapter 5 help you negotiate the best deal for all concerned—for both your client and you—the deal that leaves your profit margin intact.

Unfortunately, all sales stories don't have happy endings. When you run into difficult buyers, the tips in Chapter 7 can help you keep your sanity—and protect your time. And when selling to senior executives, you'll need to modify your approach from the very beginning, as described in this chapter.

Unless you're in an organization that hands you a fistful of leads each week, you're probably going to need to market yourself and generate your own prospects. If so, Chapter 8 provides valuable tips on ways to keep your pipeline pumping. As a sales or customer service manager, you also may find the information in Chapter 8 helpful in coaching those in a sales support role. This chapter provides tips on generating leads, up-selling, and cross-selling.

You'll notice from the "tips" layout, this book is intended to be read in any order. If you're currently having trouble with a difficult buyer, you can go directly to Chapter 6 for applicable coping techniques. If you want ideas for approaching the CEO of a new prospective organization, start with Chapter 7. If you have an invitation to speak at an upcoming industry meeting and want to turn it into a spectacular marketing opportunity, open to Chapter 8, pass GO, and collect $200.

Or, if you prefer, bring up some of these tips in your regular sales meeting. For example, you could bring up for discussion how best to plan a team proposal presentation or a new system for recording case histories to use in your standard presentations and consultative dialogues.

In any case, those who excel in any field do so because they continually upgrade their skills and take responsibility for their own learning. Like Grant Thompson headed for an awards presentation in Hawaii, winners are always working on their game. Sales superstars prove no exception.

1

PROSPECTING

Managing Your Pipeline, Time, and Territory

Prospecting rarely sets off peals of excitement among salespeople. Why? Some think it takes time away from "real" selling, that it's boring, that it involves more rejection than the typical sales call, and that it necessarily equates to cold calling.

Granted, prospecting *does* take time. But if you don't do it, eventually, your real selling opportunities will dry up. Because prospecting involves discarding the uninterested, rejection becomes part of the process. Changing the way you *think* about the prospecting process, however, can dramatically reduce the sense of rejection.

Successful sales professionals understand that prospecting keeps the leads flowing, which keeps their pipeline full and their commission check fat.

QUALIFYING YOUR PROSPECTS

TIP 1: *Recognize and Discard Your Weakest Prospects*

The following criteria should be considered when you cull through the universe of prospects and try to decide where to spend your time. Make your first cut by weeding out those least attractive as buyers:

- Those where there's opportunity only for small sales
- Those with limited or no opportunity for repeat or add-on business
- Those who are not influential as part of your client list
- Those who can't give referrals for whatever reason—for example, no sphere of influence
- Those in a declining business, market, or area
- Those who are expensive and time-consuming to reach with your marketing or selling efforts

Weed out the weakest prospects so you have time for better prospects. You're looking for those who need what you have to offer immediately, and who can produce the best payback for your selling time.

TIP 2: *Profile Your Best Prospects So You Can Focus Your Efforts*

Use the following criteria to identify your best prospects and to focus your first efforts:

- *Age.* Are these prospects the target age to use your product or service? How long will they be in that age bracket?
- *Industry.* How large is the industry?
- *Education.* Is this the target educational group?
- *Tenure in business/job.* Have these prospects been in the job the appropriate length of time to need the product or service?

- *Job title.* Are these prospects in the target positions to use your product or service?
- *Urgency of their need or desire.* How ready are they to buy?
- *Uniqueness of your "fit" to their need.* Is your offering perfect for them? Can they get their needs met elsewhere?
- *Frequency of buying.* Do they buy often enough to make selling to them profitable?
- *Typical order size.* Do they order enough to pay for the effort of marketing and selling to them?
- *Size of customer base.* Is this customer base large enough to grow your company? If a business, what's the employee population or annual revenue?
- *Attitude about quality.* Are they willing to pay for the quality of product or service that you offer? Do they want a *higher-quality* product or service than you offer?
- *Money to buy.* Can they afford your product or service?
- *Visibility, influence.* Are they influential and prestigious with other groups of prospects? In other words, by selling to them, will you be able to reach additional prospects?
- *Proximity/geographic area.* Do you have (or need) physical access to them?
- *Ethics.* Are you aligned ethically and morally? There's no point in reaching them as customers and then having them boycott you because they're upset with positions your management takes about ethical matters.
- *Potential for partnership.* Is there interest in a strategic partnership for the future?
- *Openness to change/innovation.* Are you both either conservative or progressive in your thinking about products, services, procedures, processes, and policies?

These are all key criteria to consider when building a typical prospecting list. What's important to you will, of course, be determined by the product or service you sell, how you sell it, and the philosophies and marketing strategies of your own organization.

But no matter the criteria, the principle is the same: Determine *some* criteria for selecting your very best prospects from the entire planet of prospects so you can focus your time efficiently from the very beginning.

TIP 3: *Qualify Your Prospects on the Three I's*

All potential buyers can be qualified basically with questions in three categories. I call them the three I's: *Interest, Influence,* and *Investment.*

- *Interest.* Does the prospect have a need or desire to buy? If so, how urgent is that need or desire? At what buying stage is the prospect: just realizing a need; investigating options; or already evaluating options and ready to make a decision?
- *Influence.* Is the prospect the decision maker? If not, does the prospect have the power to influence the decision maker or does he or she have no influence at all?
- *Investment.* Can the prospect afford your product or service? If not now, when?

It would be quite efficient if you could e-mail prospects a questionnaire, ask them to respond on each of the three I's, sort and file, and then go your merry way.

But that would be too easy. For starters, when qualifying on interest, a prospect's typical response to anything that sounds like a sales call is "I'm not interested." A few weeks later, however, that same prospect may be searching the Internet for the very solution you're offering. That's why a more effective approach often engages a prospect in dialogue to discover or create an interest.

When qualifying on influence, the difficulty is that prospects often claim to have more influence than they do. Sometimes, it takes several interactions to discover if you're talking to the real decision maker. To complicate matters, often the decision maker is a team and not a single individual.

In addition, prospects are not always forthcoming about their investment ability. Some prospects may claim to be able to afford more than they really can, while others, as a negotiation ploy, claim not to have sufficient budget.

During the prospecting stage, you are making best guesses at determining these three issues.

TIP 4: *Prospect Deep, Not Shallow*

Don't jump to the erroneous conclusion that every "no" gets you closer to a "yes." That's true only in theory, not in reality.

If you build a shallow prospect list—with the quickest, easiest contacts to find—you may be spending your time calling all the wrong people— the shallow fish—and getting more than your fair share of no's.

Instead, it's typically worthwhile to spend more time creating a deeper, better prospect list from the start. This way, it takes *fewer* calls to get you to each yes.

TIP 5: *Leave the Door Open When You Disqualify Prospects*

When you disqualify a prospect, use wording that leaves the door open for follow-up, should the situation change, such as when more money's available; when the prospect moves into a position of greater power or influence; when there's a more urgent interest or need; or when there's a better fit for your product or service.

Examples: "With the information you've given me, I really don't think we could solve the problem you're experiencing now. I could refer you to a colleague. Would you be interested in having a name to call on that issue?" "I don't think I can offer you a good solution because of the current budget issues you mentioned." "From what you've told me, it seems like you're really fighting an uphill battle on this decision with the team as divided as they seem to be currently. Would you just like to give me a call if your situation changes?"

"So what's your take?" is a good generic closer to leave the door open. Example: "It sounds as though we may not have a good match for what you need. What do you think?" Prospects get to tell you no and save their pride.

TIP 6: *Be Aware of the Risk and Rewards of Calling Low*

The following downsides of calling on buyers too low in the prospective account have been plaguing salespeople for years:

- Buyers low in the organization often fear risk-taking and move slowly when your solution is something new to them or their organization. They fear a mistake—even if approved by higher-ups—will be a personal, career-limiting decision.
- They have smaller budgets than those up the chain.
- The sales cycle takes longer while they have to get approvals.
- They have narrower vision than those up the chain.
- Your sale often depends on their ability to tell your story to their bosses or team to get sign-offs. (Unless you write a great proposal or persuade them to let you go with them to meetings.)

The rewards of being connected at the bottom, however, can be multiplied as you move up the chain:

- Buyers at the bottom often are closer to the real need and feel the pain, so they see more urgency to make a decision.
- They can provide data to make your case to the higher-level people as to why the investment in your solution will pay off.
- They can be your in-company sponsor and provide valuable insight about who has what power and how to get around in the organization.

- They have the power to set up meetings and introduce you to higher-ups.

Consider both the risks and rewards as you determine how best to approach your targeted prospect.

TIP 7: *Be Aware of the Risks and Rewards of Calling High*

Calling at the top of your prospect's organization has its rewards:

- The sales cycle most often will be much shorter because the decision maker has authority to act.
- Executives have bigger pocketbooks.
- Executives have a vision for how your solution can affect the entire enterprise.
- Executives understand opportunity and have a greater tolerance for personal risk-taking on your solution.

Although this does seem like the broadest avenue for approaching the Promised Land, it is not without drawbacks:

- Executives may be too far removed from day-to-day operations to know there's a real problem and, thus, a need for what you offer.
- Executives may be too far removed from the day-to-day operations to feel the real pain of protracted waits while they juggle priorities and delegate decisions to tasks forces or committees.
- You may run into a political wall: The executive already has a favorite supplier or relationship in the works and says "no, thanks" to yours, killing all opportunity for appeal.
- Going over the head of lower-level people to get to top executives may alienate those beneath with whom you must work to make your project a success.

Consider both the risks and rewards as you determine how best to approach your targeted prospect—even when it looks like pay dirt.

REACTIVATING INACTIVE CLIENTS

Your best prospects may be past customers. While some salespeople treat inactive clients like stale bread, these inactive accounts may be your quickest source of new sales.

TIP 8: *Apologize to Customers Who Stopped Buying Because They Were Dissatisfied*

If past customers were dissatisfied, accept responsibility for the bad experience and apologize sincerely. Tell them how things have changed, and ask what you can do to earn a second chance at their business.

TIP 9: *Update Customers Who Stopped Buying Because Their Situation Changed*

Stay in touch, even if there's no immediate need. Have you added new products or services since their last purchase that they're unaware of? These may fit the new situation. After all, they fit your prospect profile or they wouldn't be a past customer.

TIP 10: *Remind Customers Who Stopped Buying Temporarily Because They Forgot You*

If customers have stopped buying temporarily, or if someone has simply forgotten them, ask for their business again. It may be that simple.

TIP 11: *Avoid the Typical "I'm Your Replacement Rep" Introduction*

The typical attempt to reactivate an old account starts with a newly assigned rep calling to introduce herself. It goes something like this:

"Hi, Jack. This is Amanda Lovell with Smithson United. I'm the new account executive who's taken over your account. I was just calling to introduce myself."

"Who? What company did you say?"

If they're inactive accounts you're calling, they likely don't even consider themselves your customer. Even if they do, they don't know or remember their old account rep. If they do remember, they don't care. What's more, they care less that you're new. They're thinking: "Why are you wasting my time to call and tell me you've been assigned to call me?" You might as well call and announce that your company cafeteria is now serving a new entree or that the elevator in the west wing is malfunctioning. They just don't care.

What they may care about are the same things your other prospects and customers are interested in—what you can offer them.

Here's an opening with a more subtle reference to the past, but yet a focus on a future benefit: "Ms. Clayton, this is Tony Gladstone with Quaxton. We've provided courier services to you in the past on several occasions. I was calling to let you know that we've expanded the kind of services we offer now so that we also transport larger shipments of. . . ."

RESEARCHING FOR PROSPECTS

TIP 12: *Evaluate Your Phone Presence*

When on the phone, consider three criteria: tone, vocal variety, and spontaneity.

Spontaneity stands in a category by itself as a measurement of phone presence. It refers to your ability to interact on your feet—or seat—to depart from your prepared phrasing to listen to what prospects tell you and respond accordingly.

I recall having difficulty ordering wallpaper online during a recent remodeling project. When I called the 800 number listed on the company's Web site and told the salesperson about the difficulty with the search for my wallpaper pattern, she went into a spiel about their pricing structure and guarantee. Each time I repeated my question, she continued about the quality of their paper and their guarantees. I finally had to ask bluntly, "Are you listening to my question?" to break her focus on the usual pitch and get her to give me a logical answer to my question.

Both tone of voice and word choice reveal your attitude: warm or cold, friendly or haughty, personal or impersonal, indifferent or interested, energetic or tired, enthusiastic and confident, or bored and timid, aggressive and argumentative, or open and willing to listen. It doesn't take a potential buyer long to determine tone; just a moment or two, sometimes even a sentence or less.

Your vocal variety includes pace, pitch, inflection, and volume. Pace is how fast or slow you speak. The ideal range for sales professionals is about 150 to180 words per minute. If you spoke only within that range, however, it would sound boring. Be sure to vary your pace—slow it down to emphasize a key point and let your prospect reflect on it, or speed it up to toss in an off-the-cuff comment.

Pitch is another issue altogether. A high pitch sounds nervous, while a low pitch is more authoritative. To lower a high pitch, relax and breathe more deeply. To make key points stand out, pay attention to your inflection. Inflection is to the spoken word what a yellow highlighter is to a written page. Punch the words that should stand out and make the prospect take notice.

Volume can be another irritant for prospects. A loud volume often sounds blunt and aggressive, while a low volume sounds timid and unenthusiastic. Prospects often translate a low volume to mean that you have little or no confidence in your product or service. Result: Neither will they.

Energy must flow through all you say. That energy comes through in the sum total of your pace, pitch, inflection, and volume.

Tone, vocal variety (fast, slow, soft, and loud volume, speaking with inflection rather than in a monotone), and spontaneity—these three things determine your phone "presence." Record your voice. Analyze it. Evaluate carefully.

TIP 13: *Treat Gatekeepers Like Gold Mines*

A demanding tone sets the gatekeeper in motion—usually against you.

The first-name and no-company-name ploys are trite and unprofessional. Deception typically angers bosses when they ask gatekeepers how you got through. Don't alienate your only ally in the prospect's office by lying or misleading in saying the call is confidential, calling the boss by first name as if you are friends, or stating that the boss is expecting your call.

Involving gatekeepers may be the only way to get the boss's attention. Tell your story, stating the benefits and asking if they think the boss would be interested. Of course, if they say no, don't take it at face value. The gatekeepers may not always know the big picture. If you get at least a "maybe," solicit their help. Ask for the boss's extension and then leave a voicemail. Also ask them to be on the lookout for literature you'll send.

Use the gatekeeper as a coach until you get through. They know their boss's schedule, personality, pet peeves, preferences, and hot buttons. We frequently bring executives to our offices for coaching sessions, and you'd be surprised what we learn with just a few questions to their administrative assistants as we prepare for the day: from their favorite brand of coffee to their preference for skipping lunch; from their fear of missing a flight to their pet peeve of arriving at the terminal too early; from their feeling ill at ease at shareholder meetings to their being a micromanager. Where else can you find such intimate profiles of your prospects than from their assistants?

Show gatekeepers respect by your attitude and actions and you'll increase your pass-through rate exponentially.

TIP 14: *Select Strategic Times to Call*

According to research by the American Telemarketing Association, between 9 and 10 AM is the best hour to reach business professionals. Additionally, decision makers often come in early and stay late and their gatekeepers don't. During these times, they often answer their own phones, thinking friends, family, or colleagues are calling.

TIP 15: *Ask for the Sales Department*

Sales departments never screen calls. Ask the salesperson who answers which person handles decisions about your product or service. Salespeople always try to be helpful, right? They will transfer you to the correct person immediately.

TIP 16: *Call the General Number and Ask for the Assistant of Your Prospect*

This advice comes in handy if you run into an organization with a policy not to give out anyone's name when you only ask for a person by position or job title.

TIP 17: *Leave Succinct, Informative Voicemails That Promise Value for a Callback*

State the purpose of your call and a benefit to the prospect calling you back—specifically. Slowly and clearly repeat your name, organization, and phone number. Write the number as you speak it to keep yourself from rattling it off too quickly. Nothing irritates a prospect more than having to play back your message three times to catch your number. Unless highly intrigued, most people won't work that hard.

Imagine your prospects calling in from the airport between flights to pick up their voicemails. Seven voicemails, 18 minutes of listening pleasure, right? Wrong. Keep your message to 60 seconds or less. Don't guess; time yourself. If you ramble in your voicemail, prospects will hesitate to return your call for fear you'll do the same thing—or worse—in real time.

TIP 18: *Analyze Your Opening Lines*

"Are you having a good day?" Prospects know you didn't call to ask about their day and will stay on the line only if they have spare time. If they say no, they're focused on a negative. "Is Ms. Graham in?" Gatekeepers will seldom answer this with a yes until they know who you are and why you're calling.

"How's the weather out your way?" This is another time waster. They know you didn't call to ask about the weather and will stay on the line only if they have nothing else to do. How likely is that?

"Could I have a few minutes with you?" They're thinking either "no" or "it depends." A no closes the door, so you might as well state your agenda to answer the "it depends."

"I was in the area and thought I'd drop by." The assumption is often that you must be inefficient or desperate, or both, to have such an unplanned day. Unless you call on prospects with loose schedules, it also shows disrespect for their time.

"I'm calling from my cell in the lobby. May I come up?" Ditto on the previous reasoning.

"I was just calling people in the area who might be interested in. . . ." People don't want to feel as though you plucked their name off a list or out of a directory. They'd prefer to think you are calling with a message of special interest to them.

"I'd like to show you how to cut your operating expenses in half." Prospects typically reason: How could you? You haven't even asked me about my situation. How arrogant to make that assumption. You probably won't listen about other things either.

TIP 19: *Never Ask: "Have You Heard of Our Firm?"*

If prospects say yes, you're in the awkward position of telling them about your company anyway, which wastes their time telling them what they already know. If you tell them again, it implies that you didn't listen to what they said. Your "retelling" also assumes that they don't know the right things about your firm, so you're setting them straight.

Instead, ask: "What do you know about our firm?" This allows the prospect to talk so you can verify understanding. Then you need only correct misunderstandings and "fill in the blanks" about important things that lead them to the relevant point you want to make.

TIP 20: *Introduce Yourself with a Benefit Statement*

Typical introduction to avoid: "This is Kyla Jefferson with Fastex, Inc. We're one of the largest manufacturers of sporting goods."

Better: "This is Kyla Jefferson with Fastex, Inc. We work with retailers to market their sporting goods line to catch the eye of today's teens."

Typical introduction to avoid: "This is Eric Anderson with Booher Consultants. We offer communication training in such areas as sales presentations, proposal writing, business writing, customer service, and interpersonal skills."

Better: "I'm Eric Anderson calling from Booher Consultants. We help managers increase the productivity of their sales teams by improving their communication skills. Specifically, we help them organize and deliver more effective sales presentations and write winning sales proposals. . . ."

TIP 21: *Slide a Credibility Builder into Your Introduction*

As soon as your prospects hear the introduction and it registers "This is a sales call," the next questions pop into their mind: "Why should I stay on the line? Is this somebody worth listening to?" You'll need to answer these unasked questions quickly and smoothly in your opening sentence or two.

Credibility builders include prestigious clients, a media link, a new patent granted, an award won, or a referral by a trusted colleague. To work such a credibility builder into your opening benefit statement without sounding arrogant—and make it sound smooth and coherent in the conversation—takes some thought. (This is why I recommend carefully planning your script rather than ad-libbing.)

TIP 22: *Add an Interest Generator to Your Introduction*

Your opening has to flow from your credibility builder to the interest generator without much hesitation, because your prospect is still thinking: "Okay, so this person might be credible, but is what she is offering relevant to me?"

Examples of interest generators: "Congratulations on the mention in XYZ article. I liked your comment about Z because that so closely aligns with what our company is doing in this area." "Linda Gibson suggested that I call you because Y." "We've just finished an industry survey and turned up what we think are rather fascinating numbers about X, a problem that several companies in the industry have mentioned as a huge challenge right now." "We've done some work on employee retention programs for ABC company with great results."

TIP 23: *State Your Purpose—Don't Piddle*

Even after an intriguing opening, never leave your prospects wondering about the point of your call. If you wander all over the place in your opening, you may keep prospects on the line once, but they may never take a second call.

At the close of your introduction, state the specific purpose for your call: "I wanted to set an appointment to drop by and discuss the survey results to see if you might be able to use this data with your own department." "I was calling to invite you to stop by our exhibit booth next month in Boston." "I would like to get your permission to add you to our mailing list for this newsletter and then call you back in a couple of weeks to discuss. . . ."

As soon as you state the reason for your call, pause briefly, but don't expect an answer. (See Tip 24.)

TIP 24: *Ask about the Prospect's Needs or Situation*

After you've stated the purpose of your call, the prospect may still be on the fence about whether he's interested enough to set an appointment, attend your trade show, receive your newsletter, enroll in your free educational seminar, etc. Don't expect a response at this point.

Pause, change the pace, and switch into question mode. You've made about four statements to this point—enough to introduce yourself and your organization with a benefit, establish credibility, generate interest, and state your purpose. Now you need to hear from your prospect and make a personal connection, giving time to decide to respond positively.

Examples: "Is this an issue your organization has also been grappling with recently?" "Has your organization done its own survey along these same lines to identify what your own engineers will be looking for in the way of new equipment over the next three years?" "Would you tell me a little more about your situation there?" "How do you handle the X issue currently?"

Depending on the prospect's answer, you should have a discussion going at this point and both of you can decide whether it would be to your mutual benefit to follow through on your stated purpose at the outset of the call. Finally, close the research call to get what you want and advance the sale to the next step.

TIP 25: *Avoid Being Overly Familiar*

Don't assume everyone wants to be called by their first name. Listen to how prospects answer their phone: First name? Last? Both?

Take care with slang, colloquialisms, or political comments. While popular phrases may be common vernacular with your best buddies, they may not sit well with the total stranger you just interrupted in the middle of a major project.

TIP 26: *Overlook Typical Sales Resistance*

People hear so much unfocused marketing hype that they automatically tune out anything they perceive as a sales message. Responses seem robotic: "I already have a CPA." "I just had my wills reviewed." "We're not in the market for vacation property."

Expect such responses and prepare what you'll say to get the prospects to really hear you. It's a good idea to restate what they've said to you to show that you've listened, but do point out the value in meeting or talking with you anyway: "I understand that you've just had your wills reviewed, but sometimes there's value in getting a second opinion on . . . , or hearing alternative approaches to . . . , or having updates about the latest research. . . ."

TIP 27: *Be Organized When You Call*

Nothing irritates prospects more than having their day interrupted to ask if they're interested in what you're offering, and then hearing you say that you don't have the information they ask for at hand. Anticipate questions you'll likely hear.

Be ready to walk prospects through your Web site. Have your database open so you can e-mail buyers an attachment quickly while they're on the phone. If they refer to a project you completed for them two years earlier, have your hands free so you can quickly access their records. Have order forms or information-request forms nearby.

If prospects have to repeat themselves or wait while you scramble, you've created the wrong impression.

TIP 28: *Use Tentative Wording*

Even though you've heard them called "weasel words," effective opening comments often include such phrasing as *might, possibly, should, in many cases, according to our research, depending on your situation,* and *of course.* Declarative statements that make definitive promises beg the prospect to doubt or argue. For example: "We can show you how to cut your utility bills by 25 percent or more." How could a caller possibly know that when calling on a prospect for the first time? Such an arrogant statement causes prospects to slam down the phone.

Softer words mark you as a credible, reasonable person who knows that situations vary. You can then transition to ask prospects specifics about their individual situation.

Example: "According to our beta-sites, this software can speed up processing time by 65 percent, depending on exactly how you have your data entered now. May I ask you a couple of questions to see if you could possibly benefit from this 'upgrade'?"

TIP 29: *Avoid Jargon with Nontechnical Prospects*

If beauty is in the eye of the beholder, jargon is in the ear of the listener: "Hello. This is Carlos Martinez from Avery Benz, E-P-X Division. I was calling to notify some of our past customers, who we haven't done business with in awhile, that we have a special shipment of VT cells, both two-ply and four-ply, coming in next week. I wondered if you might want to check your inventory and compare our prices?"

"Uh, what kind of cells?"

"VT cells. Two-ply and four-ply. I could send you our specs on them. They're made by Lambert. I think they're even better than the Hognaut K12s because they have sprockets. I know Lambert's 820 line is better. Much better. Why don't I send you a FT on it and you can look it over? I'll just fill out a 1036 so they won't generate an invoice when they ship it. You could have your engineers review it, and I'll give you a call back on Friday. How's that?"

No kidding. Salespeople do it all the time—with company divisions, supplier names, forms, technical terms, product lines, model numbers.

TIP 30: *Never Ask Prospects What They Do*

With easy access to the Internet, there's simply no excuse for calling a prospect and asking: "What exactly does your company do?" Such a question means: "You weren't important enough for me to take time to check your Web site."

TIP 31: *Listen Rather Than Pitch*

As soon as you feel that you've hooked your prospects' interests so that they will talk, let them. Ask a question about their situation or needs and listen. They will not buy from you until you listen to their concerns or questions and address them.

TIP 32: *Leave Messages from the Wild Blue Yonder*

As a frequent flier, I overhear a lot of sales professionals on the phone with their prospects and customers. When I observed the first few making long-distance calls from the beaches of Hawaii, Mexico, the Philippines, or South Africa, I was shocked. Don't they know how expensive it is to call from here? The messages typically go something like this: "This is Harold Hopkins with Universal, Inc. I'm currently out of the country, but I was thinking a little more about your situation and I think. . . ."

Call after call after call on the credit card. Then one day I commented to a caller about his being an excellent time manager. "Well, that's a side benefit. But the real reason I do it is that it impresses them. It's still different enough to make them feel important."

Which prospects and customers deserve a voicemail from an unusual place—from your vacation location, from a getaway weekend resort, from your busy tradeshow floor, from home when the rest of the city has shut down because of inclement weather? Try it; they'll like it.

TIP 33: *Leave Messages When You Should Be Sleeping*

Even if you don't want to be bothered to call from exotic or inconvenient locales, you can accomplish almost the same effect by leaving voicemails for your customers and tough prospects at odd times—late at night, on the weekend, on a holiday. They may feel that your hard work, more than that of your competitors, deserves their business.

TIP 34: *E-mail to Request a Phone Conversation*

If you've already made a couple of calls to a hard-to-contact prospect and have not received a return call, try e-mailing to set an appointment for a phone conversation. Use a straightforward subject line ("Request for a Phone Conversation"), and in your e-mail suggest several different times in the next week or two (list both your time zone and theirs so there's no confusion).

Why will this work when a voicemail may not? People listen to their voicemails and delete them, possibly intending to return your call, but they forget. An e-mail, on the other hand, can sit in their in-box for days unread—and still remind them.

TIP 35: *Develop a Response to "I Never Buy over the Phone"*

With the advent of the Internet and online shopping, this mind-set has been fading fast, and argument will not change it. The meaning of this comment is: "I don't know who you are, and I don't trust the legitimacy of your business."

An effective response: "I understand that you may not be familiar with my organization. You may have passed our office location at 444 Riverside Drive. In any case, I'd certainly be happy to make an appointment or perhaps call you back after you've had time to check out our Web site at XXX. Actually, what I was calling about was. . . ." (and proceed as you normally would).

This brief interlude gives them time to pull your URL up on their screen. At the least, it communicates to them that you do have a physical address they can verify. And you have asked for an appointment. If the rest of your call interests them, then they can verify your legitimacy in the interim.

TIP 36: *Develop a Response to "Your Product/ Service Won't Help Us"*

This comment generally represents a closed attitude to *any* solution—not just yours. If the prospect's tone sounds "friendly, but resigned," you may try a probe to verify whether the comment represents a condition or an attitude: "That sounds like a serious situation. Most organizations we run into are keeping their options open for good ideas to cut costs or grow their revenues. I've got a good listening ear. Why do you feel that your situation is so hopeless?"

Of course, you want the prospect to respond with a comment to explain that's not what was meant. You've engaged in dialogue to explore possible opportunities.

TIP 37: *Develop a Response to "We're Declaring Bankruptcy"*

Respond with: "Sorry to hear that." Immediately express concern about the prospect's personal situation: "I hope this won't affect your personal job security. Has the organization notified the various divisions about any groups that will be laid off?" Such a reaction from you will tend to establish a personal connection before you try to go further with your call.

Next, you can gradually return to the purpose for your call: "Actually, the bankruptcy proceeding may be just the protection you need to get traction and make the appropriate adjustments in your operations. Will you continue to operate X (or offer Y or need Z) during this time?" If the answer is no, probe further about the appropriate time frame to check back to see "how things are going with them personally."

It's often during such difficult times that you can get your foot in the door by expressing personal concern for prospects when there's no business to be gained. You then check back a couple of months later to see if they've held on to their job and "if their business is doing better." Believe me, they'll remember you when times get better and they're ready to buy—or when they move to a new position in a new organization.

TIP 38: *Develop a Response to "We're about to Merge (or Be Bought Out)"*

Respond with: "So what's your view on that—a good thing or a bad thing? How will it affect your own job?" Most people respond to a friendly expression of concern for their personal well being.

(Refer to the previous tip for additional explanation.)

TIP 39: *Develop a Response to "I'm Leaving for a New Job at the End of the Month"*

Their mind is not on the current job, so you'll fare better by responding first with interest in them as an individual: "That sounds exciting. Within the organization or to greener pastures elsewhere?" Show genuine interest and wish them well. Most will warm up to your willingness to take the time to engage in dialogue about their future.

Then transition to ask about their replacement: "Well, I'm sure you're leaving things in good order in your current job. Can you give some good advice about who to contact as your replacement and what the best time frame might be?" After you've established the personal link, many will likely make the effort to link you with an appropriate person.

The absence of someone in the current "correct" level also can be a great excuse to call on someone at a higher level in the organization. If you've established quick rapport, ask: "Until they fill this position, who would you suggest I talk to at the next level in the organization?"

TIP 40: *Develop a Response to "I'm New to the Job and Need Some Time to Get Settled In"*

Respond with personal attention: "I understand. Congratulations. Are you new to the entire organization, or just this position?" That's a closed question, so when they tell you where they moved from, follow up with: "So why do you think it's going to be a good move for you—what new responsibilities are you looking forward to?" That opened-ended question rarely fails to engage the prospect if you listen with genuine interest and ask intelligent follow-up questions.

Transition with: "So what do your plans look like for the next few weeks?" Then listen to their priorities and for hidden opportunities where you might help. Your goal is to convey to them that you can help them get a fast start: "We love to consult with people just moving into a new job because we think we can offer some 'quick start' suggestions and save them some headaches and time in X." Continue with your typical opening to create interest.

Even if they ask you to check back after a few weeks, you will have begun your relationship on a personal note, with an invitation to investigate future business needs.

TIP 41: *Develop a Response to "How Do I Know This Isn't a Scam?"*

Respond with: "I understand that you may not be familiar with my organization, so I'd be happy to provide references for you. If you'd like to refer to our Web site, our URL is <www.___.com>. You also may be familiar with our office located on I35 at the Preston Exit.

"In any case, if you'd feel more comfortable talking face to face, I'd certainly be happy to make an appointment." (If you don't actually want to make an appointment without qualifying the prospect first, just continue without pausing for an answer.) "Actually, what I was calling about was. . . ." (and proceed as you normally would).

You've now added credibility to your faceless phone call in several ways: you've directed them to your impressive Web site; you've provided your organization's physical location; you've offered references; you've offered an appointment; you've been patient and courteous.

TIP 42: *Search Standard Resources for Prospects*

You can find both print and electronic directories with names of individuals, businesses, and organizations, often searchable by standard industrial codes, city, state, size, job title, and so forth. Here is a list of the major references at your disposal:

Internet

- Prospect company's Web site
- <www.bigyellow.com> (businesses by category, city, state)
- <www.hoovers.com> (company profiles)
- <www.worldpages.com> (provides Standard Industrial Codes)

Directories

- *American Society of Association Executives*
- *Directory of Associations*
- *Directory of Directories*
- *Dun and Bradstreet Reports*
- *Dun's Million Dollar Directory*
- *Encyclopedia of American Associations*
- *Encyclopedia of Associations*
- *The National Trade and Professional Associations of the United States*
- *Standard and Poor's Corporate Records*
- *Standard and Poor's Directory of Corporate Affiliations*
- *Standard and Poor's Register of Corporations*
- *Standard Rate and Data: Direct Mail Lists*
- *Thomas Register of American Manufacturers*
- *Value Line Investment Surveys*

Public Information Records

- *Catalog of United States Government Publications*
- *Monthly Checklist of State Publications*
- Business-to-business directories
- Property tax records
- Quarterly, annual, 10-K reports
- Residential directories
- Street address records

TIP 43: *Use "Change" Lists*

You can buy lists or compile lists of people making changes in life or business, or who may be in a new situation where there's a likely match for your offering, such as a new job, marriage, divorce, birth, move, hospital admission, new home, or other various licenses or certificates granted.

TIP 44: *Buy "Call" Lists*

You can purchase call lists of individual prospect names from list brokers or direct from the individual people or companies who have compiled them. Such lists often are created from respondents to other sales campaigns.

The company may or may not tell you how the list was created, but you can always ask. This information can help you decide which lists to buy among the many available. Also, be sure to ask how often the list is updated.

Other key questions to ask: What format is the list offered in—CD-ROM, electronic, mailing labels, printed hard copy? Can you create your own list from this purchased list? How is the list organized—by job title, geographic region, size of company, response to other offers?

You don't want to waste precious prospecting time on bad lists—especially those for which you've paid good money!

TIP 45: *Buy in Small Chunks*

Most companies require that you order 5,000 names at once. Because lists become outdated fast—in about 30 days many of the names, numbers, and addresses have changed—never buy until you're ready to use them. (An exception to this high turnover, of course, is lists of those in executive positions, which tend to be accurate for longer periods.)

If you're purchasing the list yourself, you may want to organize several of your colleagues in a calling campaign and make use of the list together.

TIP 46: *Vary Your Calling from Back to Front*

This applies to both purchased lists and your own internal database. The tendency is to always start at the front, which means the people at the end get fewer calls.

TIP 47: *Give Yourself All the Creature Comforts Possible*

Use the right equipment. A headset reduces fatigue and keeps your mouth the correct distance from the phone. It also allows you to work hands-free so that you can make a computer record at a moment's notice or jot a quick note as you move down the list.

Also, hang a mirror nearby so you stay aware of your facial expressions and vocal energy. Your caller can hear your smile. If you don't believe that, notice the next time someone calls you. Listen to their voice and see if you don't envision their facial expression while they're talking.

TIP 48: *Get a Room with a View*

As long as you're not entering notes on your computer, consider standing up. If you're tired of a "desk job," looking at the same four walls, make yourself "portable" at least an hour or two a day. If you work from a home office, as more and more salespeople do, you can place your call list on a counter or tall stool in front of a window with a great view.

Posture and voice are almost inseparable. Your prospect hears either a tired voice or an energetic voice. That voice flows from your body position, posture, and movement. If you want to sound alert, look alive.

TIP 49: *Write a Script for Reference, but Don't Read from It*

People who resist having a prepared script insist that they want to sound fresh and not canned, natural and not unnatural. That's EXACTLY why you need an excellent script. When you see friends or family face to face, you sound natural because you're relaxed and you get feedback from them.

When you call a prospect, you don't sound as natural for the same reasons—you can't see them, you get little or no feedback, and you're not relaxed. That's why you may start to ramble and sound nonsensical and strange. Preparing and *practicing* an *effective* script actually does make you sound more natural than if you were speaking, well, naturally.

Above all, make a script "your own." The following three steps can help you do that:

1. Write a script that includes the key points you need to get across in your opening.
2. Talk out the script until you perfect it with your natural cadence and word choices. Edit the script, substituting your own words, sentence fragments, and sentence patterns, including contractions and colloquialisms.

3. Rehearse the script until you can remember it easily with just a few glances. Consider the script polished phrasing for key talking points.

A perfect script makes you succinct and credible. Try a few calls, and then create two or three scripts. Keep records of which works best and all the variations, depending on the prospects' responses and questions.

TIP 50: *Acquaint Yourself with the Law Regarding Prospecting Calls*

You should also review the rules and regulations regarding cold calling individual consumers by checking the Federal Communications Commission (FCC) Web site at <www.fcc.gov/cgb/consumerfacts/tcpa.html>. To Learn more about the Do Not Call Registry, review the latest information at <www.ftc.gov/bcp/conline/edcams/donotcall>. Business solicitations are unregulated, but certainly you don't want to knowingly generate ill will for disregarding special requests to discontinue calling a specific business.

TIP 51: *Don't Hang Up between Dials*

You'll save several seconds between each dial. Never disconnect, however, before your prospect does.

TIP 52: *Make Notes Only about Follow-Ups*

Don't take time to jot down meaningless information such as "wasn't in" or "spoke to her assistant and she said to call back when he returns from vacation." It's best not to enter contacts into your database until you know if you have a real prospect.

However, some notes and prospects from the list would be meaningful to capture in your database—even before you speak with them. For example: "Assistant said he'd be interested. Just left for nine-month assignment in Europe. Try again in October before new project."

TIP 53: *Use Colored Dots/Ink or Highlighting for Quick Notes*

Make temporary notations during your prospecting session. For example, place a green dot by the names of those you spoke with and who asked you to send literature and follow up in two weeks. Put a blue dot by those who have no immediate interest but asked you to check back in three to six months. Scratch through names that are not good prospects at all, and leave unmarked those prospect names that you couldn't reach and that you need to try again the next time you call through the list.

At the end of your calling session, you'll enter into your database only those prospects with green and blue dots.

TIP 54: *Batch Calls to Keep Your Rhythm*

"Batching" calls in 45 to 60 minute sessions, rather than making a few here and there throughout the day, helps you establish a routine in wording and recordkeeping. "A few here" and "a few there," if you're not careful, soon becomes two here and two there, and then finally none at all.

Reward yourself at the *end* of a call session, but never in the middle. Otherwise, you'll lose time and become distracted.

TIP 55: *Keep Records on All Call Campaigns for Later Reuse*

When you call to introduce a new service or a special discount, that series of calls is a campaign for which you'll want a special script as reference. Record what worked well or didn't (including wording and approaches—calling first, then mailing, or the reverse), so that you can retain or modify the approach for later reuse.

TIP 56: *Keep Records of Unique Approaches Used with Key Prospects*

Occasionally, I work from my home office rather than going into my corporate office. When I do, I get my share of telemarketing calls. The following call intrigued me:

"Hello," I answered.

"Yeah . . . Uh . . . hold on a minute, please, would you?"

"Who is this?

"This is Mark." I didn't recognize the voice, but I waited. "Just a minute. I lost that scrap of paper. Okay, I got it somewhere. Here in my wallet I think . . . Hold on, sorry. . . . Yeah, I'm calling Vernon back."

"Mark who?"

"I got it here—just a minute. I wrote his number down. He said it was Vernon."

"Mark, he's not here. Can I—?"

He clicked off the line. The click and the fact that he didn't give me a last name were my only clues that I wasn't talking to a long, lost repairman.

A few weeks later, again at my home office, the phone rang.

When I answered, the caller began, "Yeah . . . Uh . . . hold on a minute, please, would you?"

"Who is this?

"This is Mark." The voice sounded vaguely familiar. I waited. "Just a minute. I lost that scrap of paper."

A couple of days later, same caller, same opening. Two weeks later, another call, same voice, same opening. Evidently, it had been effective to disarm people in their unthinking response, and it definitely sounded unscripted. I can typically spot someone reading a script by the second word.

His mistake: Poor recordkeeping and not being courteous when someone responded.

TIP 57: *Sidestep Manipulative Questioning*

It seems almost ridiculous to write about it in today's environment—except that I still receive such calls weekly: "I was wondering if it might be more convenient to set up a meeting on Tuesday morning or Thursday afternoon?" "What do you mean you're not interested in employee leasing? Don't you want to save money?" "If I could show you how to double your revenue in the next 90 days—guaranteed—would you be interested?"

Such manipulative questioning puts a bad taste in even the most interested prospect's mouth.

TIP 58: *Never Lie about the Fact That You're Making a Prospecting Call*

Here are a few of the most common deceptive openers: "This is NOT a sales call. Do you have 90 seconds to respond to two survey questions?" "This is Jeremy from XYZ. We're making courtesy calls to our credit card holders to ask about. . . . " "We may have an order from you. Could you verify with me the person who makes decisions about ABC? Would that be Fred Huzzler? May I check something with him, then?"

These are trite, not clever. If your prospect has an IQ higher than a peanut, these openers anger, rather than arouse interest. If your goal is an eventual sale rather than a name and an address, be straightforward and you'll get much better results.

TIP 59: *Let the Prospect Hang Up First*

When you're dialing for dollars doing your research, speed is the name of the game. However, never hang up the line before your prospect does. When they say they're not interested, your response should be "Thank you" before you move on. Never respond with a click and a dial tone.

TIP 60: *Use Any Negative Feedback to Perfect Your Skills*

I've never made a bad sales call that I couldn't learn from.

Doing prospecting calls the first month of business, I remember using this opening line after introducing myself: "I was calling to see if you might have an interest in our technical writing workshops?" The engineering manager on the other end of the line responded, "I can't think of *anything* I'd have less interest in!" and slammed down the phone. Then I thought about it: Why would he have an interest in them? I hadn't created interest by stating any benefits or expected results.

Lesson learned: Script a "benefit" opening.

Then there was the time I called about a dozen prospects to set appointments, and every one of them said yes. The problem was that none of them was a qualified decision maker. They were too low in the organization to have authority to sign off on the dollars needed to make the purchase.

Lesson learned: Don't waste precious prospecting time and traveling time to meet with people who can't buy.

Negative feedback can be just as valuable as positive feedback.

TIP 61: *Know the Value of Each Call or Visit*

When feeling rejection, it also helps to understand the value of each prospecting call or visit. If you've selected or built your list well with qualified buyers, every effort does have a dollar payoff. You can literally forecast your next paycheck.

For example: You may close most of your sales on the phone. If you make 30 prospecting calls a day, you generate five qualified leads that enter the sales cycle. Eventually, with a few callbacks, you know you'll close three of those five sales, or one of every ten people you call.

Another example: You may close most of your sales in person, face to face. In 30 prospecting calls, let's say you generate eight leads—from those who seem mildly interested and tell you to "call back in a month when I have my new budget" to those who say "send me some literature." Of those eight leads, three will eventually set appointments to talk more seriously. You'll close one of those three and earn a $2,000 commission. Divide that $2,000 check by those 30 prospecting calls you originally made, and you'll discover you earned $67 per call.

Whatever your numbers, determine your formula and your averages to know where you stand. Then set your goals—daily, weekly, and monthly. Each call gets you one step closer to your goal.

TIP 62: *View Prospecting as a Game You Must Win to Help Customers Who Want to Be Found in the Maze*

Where there's a sales opportunity, there's always potential for rejection. And that rejection most often happens during prospecting efforts. The ability to handle rejection without taking it personally is a positive attitude of successful sales professionals.

Most salespeople who've been prospecting for awhile understand that some rejection goes with their territory, or any territory, for that matter. You'll notice that the brick wall you may occasionally hit has no hands or face on it. It's not personal. It's just there.

Prospects may reject your call for any number of reasons: They're too busy to listen. They don't know or trust you or the company you represent. They have no real need, no real desire, no urgency, no money. They hate to make a change, and staying with the status quo seems easier. Or, they may not understand the value of your product or service. Some reasons are more typical for some products, services, and organizations than others.

These rejections all have one thing in common: The reasons have nothing to do with you personally. Even where trust is concerned, that's the case because they don't know you—they haven't interacted with you long enough to get a sense that they can believe what you say, that you'll follow through, that you're reliable.

Of course, good salespeople work to overcome these rejections by listening for buyer needs they can meet or by helping buyers understand the value of their product or service.

Ultimately, however, rejection is about a situation or skill, not personality.

Even if your goal is repeat and referral business, you want to continue to prospect—just in better ponds for bigger fish.

ALLOCATING YOUR TIME

TIP 63: *Set an Overall Revenue Goal and Time Frame*

Although I played basketball from the fourth grade on, I never was one for just "shooting a few baskets." Oh, sure, when we had only ten minutes to warm up before a game, the coach had us do specific drills. But as soon as the team gathered on the court and we finished the routine drills, she had us scrimmage. The same happened on the driveway at home. When my friends came over, as soon as at least four people showed up, we chose sides and started a game. Even in play, I like the sense of accomplishing something—working to rack up points—rather than just idly "shooting baskets."

The field of selling attracts people cut from the same competitive cloth. How can you know if you're winning if you don't keep score?

But scorekeeping works best if you do it a little differently in selling. Rather than starting out with a zero-based score and counting *up* as you go, start by setting the score you want to achieve and the time frame you want to achieve it in. Then work backward to make it happen.

TIP 64: *Set Specific Objectives within Your Revenue Goal*

After you have an annual revenue goal, you know what your salary and commission check will be. To make that reality, break down that goal into specific objectives according to what makes sense for your accounts, your product and service lines, and amounts. How many repeat customers can you count on? Can you sell these repeat customers a new product or service? How many new buyers do you need to reach? List the new accounts you plan to target. What products or services are a perfect fit for their organization? What is a reasonable revenue goal for each buyer?

TIP 65: *Develop a Specific Action Plan for Each Account You Want to Target or Penetrate*

Goals without action plans and deadlines are merely dreams. You have to get specific with your plans. How are you going to reach these buyers? What's the best first approach? List two or three entry points. Who can you contact for an introduction to these new accounts? What information can you share that would be of value to them and lead to an appointment? What personal marketing steps can you begin and continue throughout the year to stay in front of these accounts? Outline what you'll do in month one, month two, and so forth. Get out a calendar and get specific.

TIP 66: *Monitor Your Numbers Religiously*

Weight trainers and sales trainers have at least one thing in common: They preach recordkeeping. Why should you take the time to monitor your selling averages and ratios? Your numbers help you identify misused, unproductive time and also help you allocate your time to see increased growth in income.

In planning your path to high performance in real time, you can't set goals for the future if you don't know your "stats" for the past:

- How many calls per day, week, and month
- How many sales presentations or discussions in a week or month
- How many sales closed per day, week, or month
- How many repeat clients
- How many multiple product or service lines sold to the same customer
- The ratio of leads to appointments
- How many proposals to closed sales
- The average volume per sale
- The percentage of total volume by client

Basically, as Jay Abraham points out in his book *Getting Everything You Can Out of All You've Got*, you have three ways to increase your sales volume:

1. Increase the number of clients you have
2. Increase the dollar amount of the average sale
3. Increase the number of times your clients buy from you

Consider what would happen if you could increase any of these areas by just 10 percent a year. Here's an example: Let's say Joanne has 50 clients. Her average sale is $7,000. Each client, on average, buys twice from her during a year. Her total annual sales volume is $700,000.

Example: Current
50 clients × $7,000/sale × 2 sales/year = $700,000/year

Let's see what would happen if Joanne had only a 10 percent increase in all three areas: 10 percent more buyers, 10 percent greater order volume, and 10 percent more transactions from each client per year. Her annual sales volume would grow to $931,700 a year, a 33 percent increase!

Increased by 10%:

55 clients × $7,700/sale × 2.2 sales/year = $931,700/year

Now, take a look at the numbers if she increased all three by 20 percent: 20 percent more buyers, 20 greater order volume, 20 percent more transactions from each client per year. Her annual sales volume would grow to $1,209,600, a whopping 73 percent increase.

Increased by 20%:

60 clients × $8,400/sale × 2.4 sales/year = $1,209,600/year

You may be assigned to one or two large national accounts and have no choice about increasing the number of clients you serve. Other salespeople may be selling products or services that do not lend themselves to repeat sales, such as cemetery plots, burial services, or wedding dresses. Everyone's situation differs, but on the whole, most people do have choices about opportunities to increase their annual sales volume.

Monitor your numbers so you can rack up the score at will.

TIP 67: *Fire Unprofitable Prospects and Customers*

Do you have prospects who are not profitable to close? Do you have customers who cost too much to keep? After you monitor your numbers, you may come to some disappointing realizations, as did The Home Depot when they fired the U.S. Government as a customer. My friend and master sales trainer Chuck Reaves (chuck@chuckreaves.com) provides the details. As you may recall, The Home Depot *donated* lumber and other supplies to the government following the 9/11 terrorist attacks. Yet, they never collected on the PR those donations garnered. Why?

To satisfy the customer, the U.S. Government, The Home Depot would have had to comply with a multitude of paperwork requirements and hiring and firing regulations. According to their spokesperson, all this extra administrative work and cultural change would have burdened their employees to the point of distracting them from doing their primary job, and ultimately would have led to lower profits.

How much did the decision cost them? In one deal alone between Maintenance Warehouse and the government, they cancelled a $25 million contract. When all was said and done, The Home Depot felt that they had come out ahead.

We have discovered the same thing with one of our past customers—a Fortune 10 client that we had served for 14 years. Each year our training evaluations were always the highest of any of their suppliers, so they continued to give us more and more business as word traveled through all divisions and affiliates of the corporation. But the more volume they asked for and the longer the multiyear contract they offered, the deeper the discount they demanded and the more customization and coordination their projects required. Eventually we decided that, all things considered, we needed to fire them as customers. While they were a prestigious organization on our client list, we could no longer afford to serve their demands at what they were willing to pay.

Look at your own numbers and the profit margin on each prospective account. Then plan your time accordingly.

TIP 68: *Separate Your Sales Goals from Your Sales Forecasting*

Don't be known as a "hip-hop host of happy hour." In bad economic times, speculating spells disaster for organizations that depend on accurate forecasts to make hiring decisions and to order from their own suppliers. Aim to set your personal sales goals to motivate yourself. Plan to exceed them, but use them as stretch goals.

Sales forecasts, on the other hand, should be accurate and predictable. If you routinely turn in inaccurate forecasts, you are lulling yourself into complacency and damaging your career. Sharp sales managers eventually will learn to discount your forecasts—even when they're for real—by the average percentage that you typically overestimate.

TIP 69: *Get in a Groove*

Set daily, weekly, and monthly routines. Everything goes better with a routine—from running Saturday errands to getting dressed for work. The same is true with your selling activities. Consider these typical time-intensive events and activities in your overall planning cycle:

- Trade shows per year
- Educational events per month
- Networking events per week
- Speaking engagements/panels per year
- Articles published per year
- Outbound calls per day
- Appointments per week
- Personal growth and training activities

Basically, you can divide all these activities into four categories: administrative work, traveling, prospecting, and selling. How much of your day do you estimate you spend actually selling? Are you sure?

Members of the Million Dollar Roundtable have been asked that same question. This organization is an international, independent association of the top 6 percent of life insurance producers worldwide, with 19,000 members, representing 400 companies from more than 50 nations. Here's how they report spending their time:

Administrative time: 20%

Traveling to appointments: 20%

Prospecting: 40%

Selling: 20%

Less successful sales professionals become overwhelmed by the paperwork, spend an exorbitant amount of time completing administrative tasks and traveling; therefore, they have less and less time to prospect and sell—the two most vital aspects of their success.

If you don't plan for things, they often happen haphazardly—or worse, not at all. Routines make sense in sales, as well as in exercise. As a salesperson and good time manager, you have to walk a fine line between being constantly interrupted and being accessible to your clients and to prospects who expect a speedy response.

The difference: planning and prioritizing with routines.

TIP 70: *Make Sure You Have Good Reason to Travel*

More and more buyers prefer to deal over the phone, even for large-ticket sales involving multiple decision makers. In our offices, we routinely are involved in conference calls with groups of three to nine committee members, residing in two or more locations, to discuss a buying decision with two or three of our sales team.

All for good reason: the cost of travel and time. Buyers know that sellers have to cover the cost of sales in their profit margins; therefore, when they insist on having several face-to-face meetings involving travel, that cost will have to be rolled into the bid for any project. Buyers, too, incur a cost when asking their committee to show up in the same room.

Phone meetings also tend to make people more efficient; chances are greater that buyers will have done their homework in reviewing the proposal or slides sent ahead of time and preparing their questions.

A final reason to use the phone or hold a videoconference rather than meet face to face is simply control—both buyers and sellers find it easier to wrap up a phone call and go about their day.

Think twice about travel. Then think again.

TIP 71: *"Warn" Rather Than Reconfirm*

What can go wrong to cause a buyer to stand you up? Let me count the ways: "Late getting out of here to go to lunch." "Crowded restaurant and late getting served." "Last appointment ran over." "In a meeting that ran late." "Had a family emergency." "Got sick last night and didn't come in this morning." "Had car trouble and didn't make it back to the office." "Still on the phone with an important client." "Has someone in her office—I'll try to get a note to her." "The lawyers are grilling him. Would you mind rescheduling? I don't think you'd want to talk to him today."

Generally, salespeople don't like to reconfirm. They're afraid if they call to reconfirm, prospects will take that as an opportunity to cancel. True, they might. But if they're not all that interested in talking, what will you gain by seeing them against their will?

A good alternative is to call an assistant and leave a message that you're confirming, without waiting for a yes or no response. This serves as a "warning" and leaves unspoken the step of someone calling you back to cancel if that's necessary.

TIP 72: *Map Your Territory When Setting Appointments*

I started selling in Houston, where there's no mass transit, there's three-hour morning and afternoon rush-hour traffic, and there are basically five business districts. That means if you're not careful to set appointments in the same business district for the same day, you can drive 30 to 45 minutes between each appointment—if you know where you're going and there are no traffic tie-ups. If your buyer wants to meet at a time that necessitates your traveling during peak traffic, your day can be eaten up with a maximum of three or four brief appointments.

Plan your prospecting calls with a map in mind. For example, when a prospect who's located in X area of town agrees to an appointment, you know that you set those appointments on Tuesdays or Thursdays in the afternoons. If they're located in the Y part of the city, schedule those on Mondays or Wednesdays so you can head in the opposite direction.

TIP 73: *Make a Set Number of Outbound Calls Every Day*

Just do it. Rain or shine. Early morning. Late afternoon. Half before lunch and half after lunch. Make 10, 20, or whatever number you've determined you need to keep your pipeline pumping. No excuses.

TIP 74: *Don't Put Your Customers in Voicemail Jail*

Keep your voicemail greeting current. People who complain about too many voicemails often don't realize they create part of the problem themselves. They do it because they fail to update their voicemail greeting daily, so callers don't know whether the "This is Dave Wilson with Universal, Inc. I'm either away from the office or away from my desk. Please leave . . ." was recorded this morning or four years ago.

If customers really need to reach you, they will leave a voicemail there. Then they will leave another voicemail on your cell phone and another in the general mailbox. They will call your colleagues and ask them to try to get a message to you in the meeting. When you finally get one of the messages and return the call, you will later retrieve the other three messages. Should you return those three also, or are they old messages?

All this confusion can be avoided by leaving a current greeting that includes your name; the date; when you'll be picking up messages; an alternative number/method of contact; and another person to contact in emergencies.

Example: "You've reached Mya Patterson. Today, March 6, I will be in and out of the office meeting with clients. I'll be picking up messages about every two hours. If your message needs more urgent attention, please call my cell phone at 817-266-1234. My colleague Wolfgang Isihabek, at extension 103, is also available to handle customer service issues."

TIP 75: *Block Uninterrupted Brain Drains*

You need time to think. You would not permit a second client to barge into a meeting while you were talking with another client. Neither should you let ringing phones nor colleagues dropping by to chat ruin your proposal-writing time or your call-planning time. Treat these administrative activities as seriously as you would a client meeting. Come in early. Work through lunch. Stay late. Do them at home after you put the kids to bed. Do them on the subway as you commute to work.

However, don't try to do them three minutes here and two minutes there. If you plan to succeed, they deserve solid, uninterrupted thinking time.

TIP 76: *Touch until Time to Target*

Another part of planning is determining how to stay in touch with those prospects further back in the pipeline—those that you can't afford to spend prime time with at the moment. Of course, you want to keep your name in front of satisfied clients, too—those who are "between purchases" at the moment because they don't have a current need. Consider these low-key occasions to give them a quick call or send them an e-mail or letter:

- Announce a new or updated model, product, service
- Warn of an impending price change and encourage them to buy before the higher price goes into effect
- Announce a staff change or a key promotion in your organization
- Congratulate your client or prospect on the occasion of a promotion, birth, wedding, achievement, or award
- Update them on an industry trend or news

- Take a quick survey of their needs, interests, and feedback, or ask about trends they see
- Offer research you've done for others that would also be useful to them
- Share or request advice about approaching an industry issue or to ask their opinion about how a process is working in their organization

Most successful sales professionals agree that you should contact prospects and clients in some way at least every three months. More often is fine if you have reason and they show no signs of considering you a pest. Six months in our fast-paced marketplace leaves too much to chance—situations change fast and a competitor has too much time to come at the moment of need and lure buyers away. "Out of sight, out of mind" has become a cliché for good reason—it happens.

TIP 77: *Determine When Hiring an Assistant Makes Sense—Somewhere between Stardom and Insanity*

Hiring an assistant when your organization doesn't pay for it can be one of the toughest decisions to make—but also one of the more profitable. You'll reach a point in your career when you're straddling the fence between stardom and insanity. That is, you may find yourself working too many hours a day to stay on top of your job because things are clicking and you're doing well, but you're riding the wave of related administrative work and it's getting bigger and bigger and harder and harder to stay on top of it.

Yet you know that if you stop prospecting, six months or a year down the line, your revenue will start declining.

The answer is not to stop prospecting. Instead, the time may be appropriate to hire an assistant or to change your work model and find a team of colleagues with whom to pool your expertise and resources.

For example, a Realtor friend of mine has such an arrangement with a colleague, whereby they share an assistant. He networks for sellers and goes after listings; she partners with general contractors and looks for buyers.

Another example: In my stockbrokerage firm and financial planning group, one team member focuses on watching the investments, a second focuses on prospecting and bringing in new business, and a third offers financial advice. They share an assistant who services the accounts and handles the paperwork.

Consider how much your time is worth an hour when you're on the phone selling. Does it make sense for you to be metering envelopes at midnight?

TIP 78: *Maintain a Well-Organized Environment*

The most successful sales professionals are the most organized. Keep what you need daily at your fingertips wherever you do business—in your home office, in your car, in your briefcase for the plane, loaded on your laptop—note cards for writing personal thank-you's, stamps, spec sheets, printed pricing sheets, order forms, catalogs, business cards to slip into a brochure, calculator, PDA, and the like.

TIP 79: *Use The SAAD Format™ for Your Internal Records*

Keep complete notes on your sales calls so you (or your manager, team, or assistant) know what has been done and what needs to be done. We teach The SAAD Format to provide an easy-to-follow structure:

- *S = Summary.* Summarize in a sentence or two the essence of your conversation.
- *A = Action Taken.* What did you recommend, send, offer, schedule, quote?

- *A = Action Pending.* What's the next step—yours or theirs? Will they send you a copy of their specs for a bid? Are they going to talk to their committee and get back to you about a date for a formal presentation? Will you call back in three weeks about meeting them at the trade show? Is your assistant going to verify space available for them to see a product demo and call back to say yes or no?

- *D = Details.* Elaborate on key details: Who? When? Where? Why? How? How much?

Recapping your calls or meetings on your database in this succinct way can save hours, keep your records easy to skim, and provide clear records that *anybody* on your sales team can understand in your absence.

TIP 80: *Make Notes Immediately on Your Detailed Discussions*

Record key interests, needs discovered, cultural issues, or potential political issues that may surface as objections. Such details fade with every passing hour. Recapping at the end of a day is dangerous. Even a two-minute recap on an envelope flap will help jog your memory until you have access to your computer for a complete record.

TIP 81: *Compile Your Team's Internal Database to Share*

Contact information may be the most widespread use, but that data is only the tip of the proverbial iceberg in a system's usefulness in tracking leads, forecasting sales, and helping you stay in touch with clients with the least effort. Learn your software package thoroughly so you can use its features to the maximum advantage. They were created with the superstar salesperson in mind.

TIP 82: *Use Alarms or Tickler Systems*

Alarms and tickler systems are reliable. Memories aren't. Call when you say you will. Such prompt follow-up conveys to prospects how you plan to service their account once they sign on the dotted line. I personally have "deselected" many suppliers based on this issue alone. If they don't call during the dating days, chances are even greater they'll forget me after the wedding.

TIP 83: *Maintain a Clean Database and Prospecting List*

You want to make sure you'll be pumping the prospects that will keep you alive and successful from a well that contains potable water. No bugs. No deadwood. No names of friends who've said "put me on your mailing list—I like to keep up to date on what you're doing." Many salespeople might be astonished how the list of "prospects and clients" receiving their e-newsletter every month actually dwindles after extracting the friends and colleagues added through the years.

TIP 84: *Keep "Deleted" Names*

You'll want to keep "deleted" names for other purposes such as cross-referencing, referrals, and client histories. This list will include people who have moved out of a job but whose records hold valuable data you'll want to use to build credibility with their replacements when hired. Some will ask never to be called and you'll need a record of those names so you don't mistakenly call them again if their name is listed on another call list. Some will have volunteered to be a reference even though they no longer have the budget to buy.

It's best to just mark these prospects as "deleted" so you don't accidentally send them "stay in touch" mail.

TIP 85: *Tag Contacts by What You Sent or What You Sold*

If you plan to leave behind a complimentary promotional item for your prospects, tag those contacts in your database with that promotion. A year later, you don't want to stop by the prospect's office and leave that same giveaway.

Also, keep records of who you sold what to within any organization. Such reminders serve well in proposals to build credibility with new buyers in other divisions. Providing this information can remove the risk of the new decision—someone else in the buyer's organization has been pleased with your product and service.

TIP 86: *Create Your Own Prospecting List*

Creating a prospecting list compiled from your own spade and shovel work will always be superior to a purchased list. This list will be tailored exactly for your offering. Hold on to the names of organizations and titles of buyers. Even if the current buyers have no need, situations change.

TIP 87: *Update Your Database or Prospecting List Regularly*

Have you ever gotten a recipe from a friend, written it on a scrap of paper, tossed it in a recipe box, and then tried to use it years later? If so, you've probably run across notations like these: "one box powdered sugar"; "two cans crushed pineapple"; "one jar olives." Powdered sugar comes in a bag now. Is the bag the same as the box? What size can? Small jar or large? Preparing the dish now becomes guesswork.

Like a gourmet cook who values recipes as a gold mine, you as a salesperson have to guard your database as your gold mine. You protect it from hackers, don't you? So don't let it rot from within. How does your database become totally useless? When you lose one prospect at a time, over the course of a few years, by doing nothing to keep it updated.

TIP 88: *Work Based on the 80:20 Rule*

During peak workloads, remember Pareto's principle: Eighty percent of your results come from 20 percent of your effort. Twenty percent of your clients account for 80 percent of your business. Focus on the high-payoff activities for your personal marketing and prospecting time.

Keep your pipeline pumping by persistence. Hot prospects usually start further back in the pipeline, so keep your eye on the entire funnel—not just on what's closing today or tomorrow.

TIP 89: *Become the "Project Manager" of the Sale*

In past decades, sales professionals prospected for new customers, handled the sales cycle, addressed concerns or objections, closed the sale, and then handed the customer off to the operations people to deliver the product or service. They popped back into the client's life shortly thereafter only to ensure that things were running well. If they weren't, they escalated the problem to a manager. If they were, they moved on and then checked back at the end of the year to take the repeat order. Occasionally, they touched base to ask for a referral.

Not any more. To be a superstar, you have to stay in touch with your buyers throughout the marketing, selling, and implementing cycles. Salespeople in many organizations today are expected to create visibility for the organization and themselves, generate their own leads, qualify those leads, lead those prospects through the sales cycle, bring together a complete team of experts to handle a complex sale with multiple buyers within an organization, close the sale, coordinate the implementation of the sale, handle any problems that develop, ensure customer satisfaction, and develop a long-term relationship with the client so that they remain loyal to the organization.

If you don't have that picture yet, broaden your view. Remember the lifetime value of your customers versus the cost to acquire them, and then reallocate your time accordingly. It's the new sales reality. If you do it well, you can reap exceptional financial rewards.

2

CONDUCTING CONSULTATIVE CONVERSATIONS

Today's sophisticated buyers like to set the pace when they purchase. As a sales professional, it's your job to structure your approach to match the seven stages buyers typically go through as they move from the status quo to make a purchase decision.

Seven Buyer Stages	Mind-set
Stage 1. Have no interest in change	They're satisfied. If you call, they don't want to talk to you.
Stage 2. Become aware of the problem, need, or desire	They may or may not listen, depending on the context and timing of your call.
Stage 3. Feel acute difficulty with status quo	This feeling becomes more acute or persistent. There's more urgency "to do something" about it.
Stage 4. Investigate options to meet need	What products or services might meet their need or satisfy their

	desire for change? At this stage, they're information collectors.
Stage 5. Evaluate options	They begin to evaluate the options and sort out their criteria and priorities: What's most important to them? What's a nice-to-have? What's a must? What trade-offs are they willing to make and at what price?
Stage 6. Decide	They decide and buy.
Stage 7. Need reassurance on decision	Most buyers feel some buyer's remorse and need reassurance they've made the correct decision.

Once you understand these stages, you more appropriately can match your selling activities to the corresponding step. Here's how your selling activities should line up with the varying buyer mind-sets:

Buyer Stages/Mind-sets	Selling Cycle Activities
Stage 1. Have no interest in change	Qualify or requalify prospect, create interest, or move on to the next opportunity
Stage 2. Become aware of need	Interview to develop need
Stage 3. Feel acute difficulty	Interview about implications and payoff
Stage 4. Investigate options to meet need	Present options
Stage 5. Evaluate options	Collaborate about choices
Stage 6. Decide	Address concerns and close sale
Stage 7. Need reassurance on decision	Reassure and lead them to follow through on their commitment to buy

Selling time is too short to waste butting your head against the wall—trying to present options (stage four of the selling cycle) when the buyer has no awareness of need (stage two of the buying cycle). Instead, you'll both be happier if you can get in step.

TIP 90: *Remember Your Doctor to Understand the Buyer's Point of View*

When you visit your doctor, what do you expect? I can tell you quickly what I abhor: No greeting by the receptionist other than "Sign in. Let me have your ID and driver's license. Just have a seat." Waiting an hour past my appointment time. The doctor coming in to ask me what the problem is, without having reviewed the charted answers to the 49 questions the nurse just asked me. Having the doctor ask questions about my symptoms without listening to my answers. Hearing the doctor order tests without telling me what the tests are supposed to reveal. Being promised someone from the office will call with test results and then having no one call. The list goes on.

When you visit your doctor, you expect a friendly greeting, courteous and prompt service, and the promised follow-up from the staff. From the doctor, you expect that he or she will ask the appropriate questions to investigate your needs and symptoms, listen to your situation and concerns, respond thoroughly to your questions, make an accurate diagnosis, present your options for treatment, lead you to evaluate the options, permit you to decide about the treatment, reassure you about your decision and to proceed with the treatment, and then help you implement that decision.

Buyers, for the most part, have the same expectations of those who sell to them. They want you to get in step and consult with them through the process: listen to their situation; assess their need, implications, and payoffs; guide them in evaluating their options to solve the problem or improve their situation; help them to decide what's best for their situation; and then reassure them about that decision.

No more, no less.

TIP 91: *Research the Buyer's Organization Before You Make the Call*

Do your homework by checking these sources: the prospect's Web site and annual report; its competitors' Web sites and annual reports; new releases by the prospect and its competitors; history of buyer stock prices; government census reports; "trend" articles in the buyer's industry journals; an examination of the buyer's products, services, stores, and distribution channels; and general directories such as *Dun & Bradstreet, Value Line, U.S. Industrial Outlook,* and *Hoover's.*

TIP 92: *Use Finesse to Determine the Real Decision Maker*

Allow influencers to save face by selecting your wording carefully as you determine the key players. You have a variety of questions to select from as you work you way through the situation: "Who can throw a wrench in your plans to convert this platform on the time line you've outlined to me?" "Is there anyone with veto power on this working agenda?" "Will you be recommending this action, or signing off on the project yourself?" "Are you and I going to need to put our heads together about each detail and get approval at a higher level, or is it as easy as having all the control rest in your hands?" "How are decisions like this made inside your organization?" "Should anyone else be present as we discuss these options?" "When the decision is made, whose budget actually pays for this?" "After you give your okay, how is the final decision process handled?" "After your evaluation, what happens next?" "Does anyone else have to give input or an okay on this before we start the work?" "Who besides you and Shannon will be involved in the decision-making process?"

TIP 93: *Never Mistreat the "Low-Influence" Person*

If you do, you're at risk for several reasons: You may have been misreading the situation; this person may not be able to help you, but often he or she can hurt you. Situations change quickly. The low-influence person may move up or on to another position where their status and needs change dramatically.

When you find you're talking with the low-influence person, don't toss them aside on a whim. Win them over, and then meet with the decision maker to summarize to them what their staff recommends. You'll need the lower-level person on your side at some point, so no need to throw hot water in their face on the way to the executive floor.

TIP 94: *Find the Dissatisfied Person in a Competitive Account*

When you're trying to get your foot in the door in a new, competitive account, look for the worker bees. You'll typically find these people in the lower echelons of the corporations—the first-line supervisors and managers, not the directors and vice presidents.

Don't sell to these low-influence people. Just call or visit to talk to them to ask how they like such-and-such equipment or service. What's working well for them and what's not working? How much is it costing them to have these problems? Who else is unhappy? How *should* things be happening? What are the acceptable standards?

Arm yourself with the disappointing data on the current provider. Then call on the decision maker higher up in the organization who has the power to change things.

Why can't organizations pass on this data themselves? They could, but they don't. I deliver dozens of keynote speeches each year on the topic of cross-functional communication. The various levels and divisions rarely talk to each other—that's why there's so much grief, and here's where you can help: Share the pain and provide the solution.

TIP 95: *Never Rationalize That the Purpose of Your Sales Call Is to "Stay in Touch"*

Buyers today don't have time for meaningless chitchat unless you're their best buddy or you're planning to take them yachting. If you're best buddies, you're probably chitchatting outside the normal workday. If you're taking them yachting, the IRS or some ethics committee probably wants to know about it.

Stay in touch through e-mail, a personal note in the mail, passing on a relevant article, direct mail, ads, industry meetings, or PR events. When you call or visit, your aim should be to advance a sale toward the ultimate closing that brings revenue in the door. Identify clearly what the next step should be. (See the related tips in Chapter 1 on prospecting.)

Where the sales cycle is concerned, never be lulled into "going with the flow"; direct the flow until it goes.

TIP 96: *Target Your Sales Call to One Objective*

Many sales professionals plan their sales calls "after the fact." That is, after they make the call or appointment, whatever happened is what they say they *planned* to have happen. But don't let what happens determine your objective "after the fact." Plan first.

By targeted objectives, I mean focus on one objective for the call or appointment. To be most useful, targeted objectives should have a single focus. Examples: "To get agreement on what's to be included in our proposal." "To ask that James introduces me to the VP of Operations." "To confirm a meeting with their committee for our team presentation."

It's easy to understand why sales professionals like to set multifaceted objectives. With several things in mind, the chances of accomplishing at least *something* increase. The problem is that that "something" may be inconsequential to advancing the sale. Such multiple objectives do provide an "escape" when the most important thing doesn't happen.

At other times, multiple objectives are the result of not knowing exactly what *should* happen. When that's the case, think more strategically. Get advice from your manager, team, or internal coach rather than waste your time and the prospect's on pointless calls and meetings.

Having multiple objectives more often than not scatters your focus during a sales call and diminishes your success in achieving your most crucial objective.

Multifocused objectives typically miss the mark.

TIP 97: *Make Your Sales Call Objective Specific*

The more specific, the better. Avoid such vague objectives as these: collect information; build a strong relationship; stay in touch; remind them we're still out here.

Instead, relate your objective to a specific step in the sales process, to a specific product or service, to a specific dollar amount, and to a specific time line. Example: "To get commitment from Jana to attend the Orlando trade show and meet with Joe Glacel about the results MacAGE achieved with our RW10 and the technical issues involved in installation." You'll notice that the objective is to get commitment from Jana to *attend*—not just to invite her. It also is to introduce Jana to a *specific* person to discuss a *specific* product and address her concerns *about technical installation issues*. The time line is implied by the dates of the trade show.

Why be so specific? There are several reasons: You can prepare questions to lead to that objective. You can focus your pre-call research more directly on that objective. Finally, you can time your sales call more appropriately—the appropriate day, week, or condition or circumstance, such as during an internal meeting when the company executives are in town.

TIP 98: *Make Your Sales Call Objective Measurable*

To be most useful, pre-call sales objectives should be measurable. That is, they should be reasonably measurable by anybody's observation. To determine if yours are measurable, ask: Will you, your team members, your boss, your internal sponsor, or even outsiders agree that your objective has been achieved? If so, how will you measure it? If you can't answer the "how" question, chances are that it's not measurable.

Examples: "To increase Glutenberg's order of GRVs by 10 percent when they reorder quantities in May" (Can you measure it? Yes.) "To discuss our new strategic partnerships with distributors on the West Coast" (Can you measure it? No. Weak objective.) "To confirm specs for the software design project to be contracted in January" (Can you measure it? Yes—you either come back with the specs or you don't.)

Working without measurable objectives is guesswork.

TIP 99: *Develop Your Unique Selling Position for Each Specific Account*

These are the typical differentiators that make a product or service unique in the marketplace. You'll notice that some items refer to the organization itself, others to service, and still others to a product itself:

- Four-hour response time
- Around-the-clock hours of operation
- Highly-qualified specialists to answer questions
- Lowest prices
- Customized solutions for each client
- Reputation as the industry leader
- Easiest to assemble
- Convenient locations
- Money-back guarantees

- Extended warranties at no extra cost
- Interchangeable, modular design
- Based on latest research
- "Think tank" of experts
- Fastest delivery
- Free delivery
- Fast decisions on requested changes
- Vast choice of colors
- Flexibility in scheduling work
- Long list of well-known, big-name clients
- Reliability, longest in business
- Stock of hard-to-find items
- Broad product line of many types, prices, styles

Once you've determined how your organization, product, or service differs from others, you've discovered your unique selling position (USP). This represents your core competency—your key strength.

You'll need to determine your USP for each individual buyer, depending on their needs, which of your products or services they require, their decision criteria, and the competitors in their situation. Consider your core strengths. Where is the match? That's your customized USP for Michael's account or Anna's account.

A generic USP won't do.

TIP 100: *Prepare Questions—Not Just Information —to Guide Your Conversation*

Questions—rather than an information "dump"—lead to discovery by the prospect. For example, here are questions we ask our prospects that lead to their discovering the need for training in developing winning sales proposals:

- Do your competitors leave proposals with your prospects when your own salespeople just walk away from the appointment and leave only a price quote?
- Do you have a proposal-writing team to prepare all your proposals, or do your individual salespeople need to know how to put together their own proposals?
- How do your proposals compare with those of your competitors? Have you ever had any feedback from clients along those lines?
- Do your buyers buy only your services and read only your proposals, or would they be comparing your proposals to those of other suppliers offering other types of products and services? In that case, how do you think your proposals compare?
- How long does it take your salespeople to put together the typical proposal?
- If we could reduce that time by 50 percent, what would that mean to you in additional selling time?
- How satisfied are you with the "boilerplate" proposals that you "cut and paste"?
- How many deals do you think you lose because of weak proposals that don't tell your story well?
- What's your current ratio of proposals submitted to closed sales?
- What would it mean to you in increased revenue if we could improve that closing ratio by just 20 percent?

For our sales presentations programs, we have a different set of questions; for customer service another set of questions; and so on.

Your questions about the situation and needs lead to answers. Those answers lead to more questions. The prospect provides more answers about the implications, costs, and inefficiencies related to those needs. Those answers lead to your telling about your solutions. Those solutions give rise to the prospect's questions about your solutions, which, of course, lead to your prepared answers, which, of course, lead to closed sales.

TIP 101: *Prepare Answers to Anticipated Questions*

If you've been selling awhile, you can anticipate questions on certain product lines and services or about your organization. You should have thorough answers. Not answers that sound canned—that has to do with poor delivery. Your content should be well thought out, clear, compelling, and complete. There's no reason to be caught off guard on a routine issue.

TIP 102: *Politely Decline to Do a "Dog and Pony" Show*

Unfortunately, buyers frequently doom themselves to uninteresting and inappropriate sales presentations and discussions that go nowhere with the generally vague invitation to come in and tell us "who you are and what you do." Such dog-and-pony shows cause you to waste time discussing things of no interest to the specific buyer or groups of buyers. If you do hit points of interest, it's often by accident. Giving generic benefits only slows down the real decision-making process. Buyers are interested in the results *they* need—what your product or service can do for *them.*

To sidestep these pitfalls—even when your buyer has asked you to deliver one of these vague monologues—consider specific questions to help you mark the trail and stay on the path: "Tell me, what do you already know about our company?" "Which issues are most important to you?" "What solutions have you previously tried to solve the problem or meet your needs?" "What options have you come up with already?" "Where do you see your biggest opportunity for growth and improvement?" "What do you hope to achieve at this meeting?" "What information would be most helpful to you right now?"

Presentations focused on your company will not likely address buyers key concerns or lead to a quick decision.

TIP 103: *Sequence the Typical Conversation in Steps*

Abraham Lincoln once remarked: "If I had eight hours to chop down a tree, I would spend six of those hours sharpening my axe." Almost anything goes better with a plan. A sales discussion or selling cycle is no different. The following six-step sequence makes sense in most situations:

1. Establish your credentials and build rapport.
2. Interview buyers on their interest, needs, and implications, and their influence on the buying decision; then listen and confirm your understanding.
3. Position and present solutions.
4. Answer questions and address concerns.
5. Gain commitment and close.
6. Follow up with implementation and reassurance.

Of course, with some products and services, the first five steps may happen in one conversation. With other complex sales involving big-ticket items and multiple buyers, you may take a year or more to lead your buyer through these steps.

The idea is simple: Have a plan. Know where you're going from the start.

TIP 104: *Dig for Original Diagnosis*

Consumers have become a skeptical crowd. If you don't believe it, watch how they flip through TV commercials, talking back to the glib announcers who promise things contrary to the user's experience. You can bet your competitors have offered similar solutions to your buyers—otherwise, they wouldn't be competitors.

And your buyers are thinking: "We've heard it all before."

To differentiate yourself in your interactions, focus on your diagnosis of the situation. Help them see their situation in a new light. Spend time asking the *right* questions—not just *any* questions. Your questions will be the most valuable part of your interaction.

TIP 105: *Avoid General Fact-Finding Questions as Icebreakers*

Examples of questions to avoid: "How long have you been in business?" "What's your product line?" "Where are you located?" "Do you have overseas operations?" "What's your annual sales volume?"

Salespeople sometimes use such questions as "warm-ups" at the beginning of a conversation, thinking these are "easy" questions on neutral ground that will "get the buyer talking" before the salesperson moves on to potentially more sensitive issues. Buyers, however, no longer have time to spend educating you about their company with general information that's readily available from lower-level staff people, their Web site, press releases, and company newsletters available in the lobby.

Break the ice with issues that are more intriguing and of higher value to the buyer. At best, such questions waste your buyer's time and your precious interviewing time with the buyer. At worse, they characterize you as uninterested, unprepared, lazy, or incompetent to the buyer.

TIP 106: *Create Urgency to Make a Change If Buyers Are Aware of a Need or Problem*

You can generally move buyers to action in one of three ways:

1. Explain that an opportunity will be lost. Elaborate on appropriate timing for the prospect to make the buying decision and be ready to support your claim. Calculate the money saved by correcting a problem, money earned by taking advantage of a sale or discount, or money lost by delaying a decision.
2. Help buyers visualize the solution—how easily the problem can be corrected or avoided.

3. Appeal to the buyer's need to feel current in the industry. These appeals create a sense of urgency to act.

TIP 107: *Create Atypical Questions to Uncover Opportunities in the Typical "No Interest" Stage*

In today's climate of lean-and-mean staffing and fast-paced work-days, even your clients may not want to talk to you. Most buyers don't have time for "relationship building" phone calls unless they're ready to make a major purchase immediately. Even then, all personality types don't enjoy chitchatting. Buyers may measure the quality of the relationship not by frequency of contact but by the efficiency with which you sell to them—the fact that you're a "low-maintenance" supplier delivering quality without requiring handholding.

So with this backdrop, any caller—beloved supplier and belated straggler—is likely to receive a "thanks, but no thanks" response. Your job is to present intriguing propositions and ask provocative questions that knock buyers off the status quo plateau.

Here are questions that may help you do that:

- "What achievement has your organization been most proud of this year? How could we push that envelope even further? What would you have to do to repeat that performance again next year in every division of the organization? Here's how we might help. . . ."
- "How progressive (or conservative) would you say your organization is? Do you agree with the way things are going? What would you like to change? Here's how we could get involved there. . . ."
- "Do you value team work, or are you more of an individualist? How so? Our goals are closely aligned. Our solutions could really help you to. . . ."
- "Are the risk takers and innovators rewarded or punished in your organization?" If they answer rewarded, follow up with: "As an innovator, if you were really going to take a risk next year and seek

a big reward, what would you set about doing? How could we support you in that?"

- "What do you think motivates people around here? What new procedures and equipment do you think your employees would like to see put in place? What problems do they want to see solved? Here's how we could help. . . ."

- "What's one of the biggest things people are complaining about around here?" (Narrow this down as much as possible to guide the discussion—after all, you don't want them to bring up the cafeteria food.) "Any big de-motivators? Here's how we could help with that. . . ."

TIP 108: *Offer Complimentary Research or Consulting to Uncover Opportunities with Buyers in the "No Interest" Stage*

When buyers have no awareness of how you can help them, you will get nowhere with "one size fits all" product or service overviews. Such statements summarize problems they don't think they have, mention investments they are unwilling to make, and promise payoffs they don't believe.

You'll need other approaches to engage them in dialogue to discover how you might be of service. Here are three suggestions to use as the basis for your phone call or meeting with them:

1. To provide research findings on industry trends and ask for their reactions and observations regarding their own organization

2. To offer data and feedback about research you've done on their company and to suggest ways they could improve

3. To offer free help, such as consulting opinions, pilot programs, or performance testing on beta products, in exchange for references

While none of the above is a new approach, what makes each unique to you is your personal credibility in making the offer, your timing, and the value of the offer to your specific buyer.

TIP 109: *Ask Specific Questions to Create Goals and Visions*

What must be changed, improved, or solved? Specific questions about needs focus buyers on the future and sometimes expands their vision.

Examples: "Do you think an automated warehouse system would eliminate some customer complaints about inaccurate shipments?" "Are you going to branch out and offer wireless services anytime soon?" "Do you have many clients asking for expanded options of delivery like we're offering?" "Have you ever thought about automating your back-office processes?" "How do you think your customers would respond to a new payment option like this credit card plan?" "Have you ever considered outsourcing your maintenance and engineering design services for the regional offices?" "If we were able to off-load some of these routine tasks and could free your own marketing staff to devote their creative energy on the new product line, how do you think that could pay off for you in launching this new product line second quarter?"

Your questions should start the wheels spinning—big time.

TIP 110: *Ask Probing Questions about the High Cost of the Status Quo*

Ask questions that lead buyers to realize how much their current situation—an unmet need—is costing them.

Example: "I understand that you have about a 15 percent error rate in pulling orders from the warehouse. How much does it cost you to re-stock those items?"

Example: "When you did your employee survey, you said that 35 percent of your employees marked 'very dissatisfied' with their insurance coverage. You also mentioned that your turnover rate company-wide was 22 percent last year, and that you figure each employee you lost cost you on average $10,000 to replace. If you consider the employee satisfaction survey as a warning signal, then would you say one-third of your employees are giving you a warning that they want that coverage changed? If one-third of your employees leave during the next year, how much will it cost you to replace them?"

Example: "With your current CRM system, what's the average response time to customers' e-mails? What's the average customer order amount? How many orders do you estimate you lose by not getting back to your customers for 48 hours?"

TIP 111: *Ask Leading Questions about the Value of Your Solutions*

What benefit could the buyer achieve? A cost savings? Faster operations? Less downtime? A bigger convenience? Quicker response to their own customers?

Example: "So that means the current CRM system is costing you about $84,000 a day in lost orders because customers get tired of waiting on confirmations and cancel before you confirm?"

Example: "If you installed an inventory management system such as ours, and could improve the accuracy of your pull rate from the current 85 percent to 98–99 percent accuracy, how much would that save you in restocking labor? How would that increased accuracy rate affect your customer satisfaction ratings?"

If you have industry data or test data to share, by all means, do so! Keep in mind that buyers believe what they hear themselves say, so give them ample opportunity to consider, analyze, estimate, and voice costs of their current problems and the value of the solutions you can provide.

TIP 112: *Ask Transition Questions to Lead to the Next Need*

You'll want to follow one issue all the way—from raw pain to cost to payoff to solution—before you move on. Transition questions bridge to the next issue and start the process all over again.

Examples: "What other issues do you think contributed to your lower customer satisfaction ratings this year?" "If we were going to redesign your employee benefits program from the ground up, what other issues do you think we should look at carefully?" "Let's say your sales staff had wireless phones. What else would they need to stay in close touch with their customers? Are there any remaining challenges or obstacles that might get in their way of meeting quota this year?"

Good transition questions may summarize briefly to show that you've heard what the buyer has said, but they also should suggest specific areas of interest and solutions you can provide. Smooth transitions allow you to discuss and offer multiple products and services during a single discussion without sounding as though you're doing a dump of all your products on the front doorstep.

TIP 113: *Rethink the Need to "Educate Your Customers"*

I often hear salespeople after a client meeting talking about how they need to "educate their customers." While their customers may need to know more about the seller's products or services, I think the far greater need is that salespeople need educating about their customers' business. Listening is the link to that education.

In survey after survey of buyers, this key complaint surfaces: Salespeople don't listen. Listening, however, helps you to:

- Understand your buyer's decision-making process
- Learn about the buyer's business, strategy, industry, goals, and politics
- Identify root causes of problems, obstacles, and feelings
- Determine if there's a match
- Differentiate your offerings from how the buyer sees your competitors' offerings

- Reinforce your credibility and differentiate yourself as an advisor/consultant by demonstrating you have listened to needs and opinions, and have not just pushed a product
- Stimulate thinking and lead the buyer to modify attitudes and decisions
- Lead buyers to sell themselves by listening to them talk about the needs and potential payoffs of your solution
- Identify missing information you need to discover
- Pick up emotional cues of uncensored thoughts and feelings of the buyer
- Make the buyer feel valued while building personal rapport

Who's getting the biggest education and payoff?

TIP 114: *Know Your Typical Talk/Listen Ratio*

Aim for a 50:50 ratio of listening to talking. On occasion, a listening ratio of 70:30 may be appropriate to allow your buyers time to tell you all about their issues. To ensure that level of interaction, plan and sequence your questions productively: Ask the right questions, at the right time, and in the right order.

It's fortunate that most people notice a talking imbalance when listening to others. It's much more difficult, however, to catch your own overdependence on telling rather than listening to buyers, and that difference can be deadly. Never worry about listening too much. The opposite—talking too much—is typically the buyer's bigger complaint.

TIP 115: *Leave Buyers Down for the Count*

Most Americans grow uncomfortable with silences. Sales professionals, however, would do well to resist the urge to fill in the blanks when their buyers stop talking. Don't feel intimidated by the quiet. Let your buyers think—they'll often add even more revealing information than they offered with their first guarded responses to your questions.

Use this favorite trick of reporters to encourage interviewees to continue to elaborate about sensitive subjects: Just pause, then count 1, 2, 3 before you pick up the conversational ball again.

TIP I16: *Leave Silences throughout the Conversation*

Salespeople have earned a reputation as "fast talkers" for good reasons: Buyers have short attention spans. So salespeople talk even faster. As a result, buyers feel pressured and quit listening even sooner. To break the cycle, effective salespeople leave plenty of purposeful silences. As a result, the length of buyer responses increases. Buyers think more reflectively and give better answers and more information about their own situation. They also ask more questions. In addition, the silences allow salespeople time to think about what the buyer has said, and about where to lead the conversation.

In general, the more silences you leave, the better the information you'll gather.

TIP I17: *Verify Feelings and Reactions Wrapped around Words*

Just like the date who promises "I'll call you tomorrow" but doesn't, buyers' messages are conveyed through more than their words. If you want to make sure you understand the situation correctly, listen to repeated statements during your conversation, and analyze the stories they share, listen to the emotion behind their words, and capture the tone behind their glib or global promises.

The message is in the emotion. Listen to the intensity to learn what they will or won't do.

TIP 118: *Listen with Your Whole Body*

Make listening an obvious activity. Look prospects directly in the eye as they talk—not with a blank stare, but with an engaged, "hanging on every word" gaze. Use supportive, but not threatening, intimidating, or controlling body language. Make sure your facial expression shows appropriate, genuine reaction to what they're saying. Give verbal responses where appropriate, and be sure to take notes.

Listening involves much more than the ears. If your buyer has to wonder if you've heard something, you didn't.

TIP 119: *Listen between the Lines for What's Said, What's Not Said, and What Can't Be Said*

Some buyers may not be at liberty—or may be unwilling—to voice certain problems, concerns, or issues with you, an outsider to the organization. Internal politics may pressure them to keep quiet about pain you could relieve. In other situations, they may not know the issues and circumstances, but don't want to admit they're "out of the loop." That, too, is valuable information. Finally, some inarticulate buyers need to be guided through the maze of information they possess to turn it into real communication and useful data. Whatever the case, listening leads to learning.

TIP 120: *Take Notes As You Listen*

Note taking benefits both you and your buyers. For starters, it strokes their egos, shows interest, and makes them feel important. It shows buyers that you're attentive to detail and conveys to them that you're not wasting their time in asking for information that they'll have to repeat again later.

For you specifically, consider these additional benefits: Note taking helps you retain more, helps you focus, helps you ask better questions and capture specifics, and helps you recap at the end of your discussion. Later, after your discussion, the notes play a key role in preparing your proposal or quote and in your negotiation process.

But you don't want to take just *any* notes. You want the *right* notes: preferences about your product or service—size, color, timeframes, delivery, features; key goals or objectives for your product or service; specific phrasing your buyer uses; personal data, such as family names, previous employers, education, hobbies; feelings expressed; and political situations, sensitivities, and taboos.

When a salesperson walks in and out without notes, buyers often chalk up the conversation to wasted words.

TIP 121: *Distinguish between Agreeing and Understanding*

Agreeing and understanding have similar "symptoms"—smiling, nodding head, supportive statements. Make sure that your buyer knows when you're communicating that you *understand* a viewpoint or issue as opposed to situations when you *agree* with a viewpoint or issue. Not recognizing this difference can lead to opposite conclusions—and big disappointments and misunderstandings.

TIP 122: *Listen for Leapfrog Opportunities*

During your discussion, listen for comments from your buyers signaling that they're looking for ways to grow their business or improve their operations. Some individual buyers and leading-edge organizations sit poised waiting for the next opportunity to leapfrog over their competition with the next big idea. They never think in small incremental steps. They're impatient with the typical 10 to 15 percent growth rates that many other organizations would be happy to report each year.

You'll hear comments such as:

- "We're different around here."
- "We find out what everybody else is doing—and we don't do it."
- "You've got an idea? I'll get you to the right people."
- "We need to talk. Let me get the right players in the room."
- "Let's brainstorm."
- "All of those ideas sound good. Let's explore a little before we narrow things down to a proposal."
- "Don't worry. If they like it around here, we can find the money."

Listen to such signals from your buyers so you understand when they're ready to make a huge investment in your offering and leapfrog to the next level.

TIP 123: *Listen for Plug-the-Drain Opportunities*

"Aren't all buyers interested in improving and growing themselves or their business?" you may wonder. Not on your life. Because sales professionals are a self-motivated group, it's hard to believe the rest of the world can remain stagnant. Nevertheless, that's often the case. Some businesses are in mature stages and do not intend to invest further to grow market share or expand. Their goal is to make their profit and loss statements look good and sell quickly. Other businesses and other consumers have any number of reasons to maintain the status quo.

Their focus is to plug the drain on current problems. Listen for phrases such as:

- "Let's get real."
- "One thing at a time. Let's get this approved first."
- "Look, this is our number one priority this year."
- "Our customers want this corrected. What do you have to help us with this situation?"
- "First things first."
- "How much does it cost?"

- "Where's the breakeven on the investment?"
- "What's the guarantee?"

Take your cue and follow their lead. They can think of only one leaking drain at a time. Focus on the first drain before you try to get them to replumb the whole building.

TIP 124: *Listen for Keep-Me-Informed Opportunities*

Listen for buyers who tell you they're satisfied with the current situation—but not convincingly. Change takes effort, and buyers tend to take the path of least resistance. They may say they're "happy with our current supplier," but they may actually mean, "My boss likes them, but I don't think they do a good job. And when I have enough time to fight the political battle, I'm going to do something about it."

Listen for comments such as:

- "We always like to keep up to date with what's out there."
- "You never know when our situation may change. Please stay in touch."
- "I'm not at liberty to tell you what's going on. Just keep me on your mailing list."
- "Things may change after October 10. Give me a call then."
- "I wish I could make a change, but my hands are tied. I may be in a better position to do something later."

Of course, these phrases sound like the typical "Don't call me, I'll call you" putoffs from a buyer who just doesn't know how to be direct. It'll be up to you to read between the lines with other information you've collected on the account, in the industry, and from competitor situations.

TIP 125: *Refrain from Presenting Solutions Too Quickly*

First, lead your buyers to clarify the cost of problems or the value of growth or improvements. Examples: "In what way does this affect how your drivers get the deliveries to your customers?" "How does this slow down your invoicing process?" "Are you concerned about the quality of the printed page?" "Is it important to you that . . . ?" "What is your opinion about X?" "How satisfied are you with the way X is handled currently?" "How critical is it to you that Z happens consistently each time?" "How helpful would it be to you if you could find a way to do Y?" "How serious is this issue?" "This doesn't seem like a critical issue to you—am I right or wrong?" "How much is this costing you currently?" "How would it benefit you if this decision were made?" "Would a product like this make your life easier?" "What gains would you have to have to make this worthwhile?"

Buyers need to feel the pain before they're motivated to invest the time, energy, and money necessary for improving the situation.

TIP 126: *Think, Ask, Listen Large*

It takes no more time, effort, or skill to sell a small solution than a big solution. If you aim small, you're going to sell small. If you think about solving big problems, you're going to listen for large opportunities. Don't limit yourself and your buyer with your own restrictive thinking.

TIP 127: *Ask What Your Buyers Know Rather Than Tell What You Know*

"What do you know about my organization?" allows your buyers to give their perceptions. You then can fill in the gaps, clarifying and correcting, if necessary. When you lead with, "Let me tell you a little about our organization," you're at a distinct disadvantage for several reasons: You're doing all the talking and setting yourself up in lecture mode as the person with all the answers. You may be providing information already known; you may be elaborating on what the buyer doesn't care about knowing; and you have no way of knowing if the customer really understands what you've said—and most important—what your organization offers.

TIP 128: *Make Sure All Conversations Benefit the Buyer, Not Just You*

Picture yourself in your workplace all day long, being approached by callers or visitors who have only one interest—"What can you do for me today?" That's the experience of many of your own buyers. No wonder they resist taking "just one more call" from someone they perceive to be selling them something.

So take a different tack from your competitors. Approach the buyer to *give* them something—an interesting new angle on handling an industry problem; an intriguing insight from an expert; new research; a new set of guidelines for judging a process; a job aid or reference tool; or personal concern and well wishes.

When you plan your calls and appointments, consider adding to your sales objective: What can I leave with them of value?

TIP 129: *Trade Information to Get Information*

Example: "We're finding that many of our clients have experienced a difficult third quarter because of the problem in getting shipments of raw cotton. What has been your experience in that regard?"

Until you have a strong relationship with the buyer, information may not be readily forthcoming because of a lack of trust. When that's the case, you have to be the one to bridge the gap by offering the first trade. Just be careful that you don't offer confidential information from other clients or sources; otherwise, your buyers may grow even more leery of putting their information "on the street" by offering it to you.

TIP 130: *Never Make Buyers Feel Interrogated*

Avoid run-on questions—multiples that buyers can't answer or that make them feel as though they're being cross-examined. With a sensitive question particularly, explain why you're asking it with a lead-in that lets them know the benefit of having an answer.

Not: "Do you know what percentages of your files in this department are never referred to again?"

But: "Most document managers report that 85 percent of their documents are never referenced again once filed. If we could identify those unnecessary files, that would represent a huge savings of floor space. What's your estimate on the percentage of such files in this department?"

Question and answers should be insightful, not threatening.

TIP 131: *Don't Ask Self-Serving Questions*

Leading and one-up questions make a sharp buyer resistant. Example: "Were you not aware that we guaranteed on-time delivery, and had you maintained your contract with us during the past three years the problems with the current vendor would never have led to the complaints from your own customer base?"

Although questions often *lead* to your point during a consultative dialogue, they should not *be* the point. The buyer will feel trapped and will resent—rather than appreciate—your insightful dialogue.

TIP 132: *Avoid Asking "Are You Interested?"*

People think an affirmative answer to this question commits them to buy. Instead, simply ask if you can tell them more about X or send them information about Z.

TIP 133: *Ask "How Did You" Rather Than "Why Did You" Questions*

"Why" questions often sound challenging and put the buyer on the defensive: "Why did you decide to do X?" "Why do you think an upgrade isn't warranted at the present time?" "Why was the décor done in navy?"

"How" questions, on the other hand, often get at the same information, but in a less challenging tone: "How did you make the decision to do X?" "How do you decide when to make an upgrade?" "How was the color navy selected for décor in this building?"

Phrasing makes a huge difference in reception.

TIP 134: *Develop Your Unique Selling Position (USP)*

How your products or services differ from your competition in the marketplace represents your USP, which is your core competency or strength. For a more complete discussion of a USP, refer back to Tip 99.

The typical differentiators that make a product or service unique include broad selection, discounts available, advice/consulting service, speedy response, convenience, add-on/turnkey services, more comprehensive warranty, expertise, value-added extras, buyer education, brand recognition, specialization, diagnostics, packaging, advertising, design/styling, distribution, centralization, financing terms, and knowledgeable representatives.

By its very definition, a USP should be one of a kind, "unique." But a "core strength" may also be someone else's "core strength" as well. When that's the case, you'll need to work harder to fine-tune your expression of that core strength.

TIP 135: *Tweak Your USP by Positioning in One of Four Categories*

After you have developed your USP, you still may find a competitor or two at your heels. Essentially, you can further differentiate from four winning positions based on that uniqueness: lower price, better quality, faster, and product difference.

This breakdown won't work in the reverse. That is, you can't start off differentiating in the four big categories (lower price, better quality, faster, product difference) and then move to the finer points as outlined in Tip 134. For example, if you position your widget as the fastest solution (quick access, quick delivery, quick assembly, quick install, and so forth), you will still have competitors—others who also offer a fast solution and who may or may not offer some of the other same distinguishing benefits that you offer.

If you eliminate competitors by saying you're the only supplier who offers X, Y, and Z and then narrow the funnel even further by providing this service cheaper, then you have differentiated to the final degree.

TIP 136: *Differentiate—Even with a Generic Product*

Differentiation is *always* possible, even with a generic product, because you and your buyer are unique: Consider your track record, level of quality, services, execution, and expertise. Avoid dwelling on strengths that are no different from those of your competition. Instead, go for the gold—your superior differences. Then match those differences to your buyer's criteria.

That exact match—where your superior strength crosses your buyer's acute need—is your USP, even with a generic product.

TIP 137: *Focus Only on Generic Weaknesses of Competitors Rather Than a Single Competitor*

Not: "Competitor B uses Dohickey Y valves in their engines, which are much less durable than Dohickey Zs that go in our engines. . . ." But: "Many competitors use Dohickey Y valves in their engines, which are much less durable than Dohickey Zs that go in our engines. . . ."

Not: "Competitor C is going to charge you much more on their daily consultant rates when you have smaller add-on projects such as up-grades and maintenance tasks." But: "Smaller companies find it difficult to locate consultants in global markets to offer the same kind of low daily rates as large companies like ours because. . . ."

Never compare to just one competitor; always do a comparative analysis with at least two or three. Knocking a competitor offends many buyers, plus it takes time away from discussing your own solutions and the buyer's needs.

TIP 138: *Avoid an Up-Front, Point-by-Point Comparison with a Competitor*

Showing a complete scorecard up front presents several dangers: You'll undoubtedly cover points the buyer won't be interested in; you may accidentally highlight areas of strength for the competitor, because chances are, your product or service isn't perfect; and, additionally, you may offend by what the buyer perceives as an arrogant tone and approach.

Generally, a better approach is to focus on your uniqueness with several blanket statements spread throughout your discussion, such as: "Our organization is unique in that. . . ." "Unlike others in the industry, we always. . . ." "We're the only company that. . . ." "Ours was the first company to. . . ." "The industry has recognized our organization twice with an award for. . . ."

Another way to position yourself against an incumbent's weakness is to ask "How do you currently handle X?" or "How satisfied are you with the Y process?" When their answer reveals dissatisfaction about a competitor's performance, toot your own horn about your strength in that area.

TIP 139: *Position against Competitors' Unique Strengths and Then Make Your Strength the Key Criteria*

For example, if your organization is small, you can grant that the market leader has superiority in market acceptance or name recognition. You can then position yourself as better able to customize or respond quickly because of your smaller size or because you have "boutique" expertise. Example: "Competitor A does have offices worldwide. Competitor B has the best dealer channel. And we have the quickest response time." Then you explain why fast response time should be the buyer's key consideration.

TIP 140: *Focus on Benefits, Not Features*

A feature is what a product or service is, has, or does. The advantage of that feature produces a benefit. Generally, buyers are more interested in the benefits than the raw features. The features are only a means to the end—the benefits. As you explain your product or service, link your benefits to features with "so that . . ." or "which means that . . ." statements.

Incorporate the buyer's words into your benefit statements, and match the buyer's level of understanding; that is, if they don't use technical terms, steer clear of jargon. How much detail do they ask about? Give it to them or omit it—to meet their interest.

Feature	Benefit
220 threads per inch	Holds up under intense wear
Stenson version 6.0 or higher	Allows you to play video and audio clips
Software analysts with 20 years' experience	Takes less time and expense to identify and correct computer problems
Locations in 28 cities	Easy access to our consultants

TIP 141: *Focus on Value after Establishing Benefits*

Benefits are assumed by the seller. Advantages and true value, on the other hand, are in the eye of the buyer beholder. Never present your product or service from a "benefits" list. Be selective about what you mention to a buyer as an advantage or "value" or reason to buy from you.

For example, a salesperson tells me they have locations in 28 cities, which means I have easy access to their consultants all around the country without having to pay travel costs when I need them on-site. But what if I have only two offices ten miles apart? That "benefit" has no value or advantage for my operations. For a salesperson to tell me about this "benefit," creates one or more of the following impressions: they don't understand my business; they didn't listen to me; they don't know how to tailor a presentation; or they're on automatic pilot.

On the other hand, if they focus on a feature, explain the benefit, and then show the value to my business—the overall results of my investment over the cost—I'm highly likely to buy. Showing the *value* of one or two benefits beats dashing through a litany of features and benefits any day.

TIP 142: *Never Save the Best for Last*

Start with your very best first. If you can't close on that product or service arrangement, then you can step down in price and benefits without insulting the buyer. Buyers are flattered when you assume they can afford the best quality. The buyer may then step back up the ladder after having seen the best.

Here's a good opening: "To appreciate the finer points of the highest quality widget, let me start by showing you the very best." You're not implying this is the only one to buy or that the buyer is making a mistake to choose lesser quality. As you move down in quality, the perception is that you'll be "saving" the customer money and offering a better deal.

TIP 143: *Guard against Turning a Sales Conversation into a Sales Presentation*

Nice people make receptive listeners. They pay attention, ask detailed questions, and let you talk. At the end of the meeting, you may realize you've actually slipped into sales presentation mode and have done all the talking. As a result, you've discovered very little about your prospect's situation, needs, or criteria for buying.

Opportunity lost. More sales happen as a result of asking than telling.

TIP 144: *Answer the Question Your Buyer Asks— Clearly, Completely*

If you've been selling awhile, you've probably heard most of the typical questions buyers ask about your products and services. That's the biggest problem in answering buyers' questions—*thinking* you've heard them all before! Buyers complain about salespeople as often as patients do about their physicians: "They didn't listen to the symptoms or answer my questions; they just told me to take two aspirin and call them in the morning."

Have you ever watched a televised press conference or a debate in which a reporter asks a political candidate a direct question such as: "Are you for or against raising property taxes?" and the candidate talks for three minutes and yet never answers the question? What impression does that leave in your mind? Willful obfuscation? Purposeful deceit? Carelessness? Fuzzy thinking? None of which is the intended effect.

TIP 145: *Don't "Overrespond" to a Technical or Complex Question*

Answer the buyer's question clearly and succinctly and then stop. Continuing to ramble on about a complex matter can make the issue seem even more complicated and can cause the buyer to give up in frustration.

Give an overview of the "must know" information, then wait to see if your buyer asks for further details. If so, you can always add a second layer of detail beneath your overview. Let their follow-up questions be the guide as to how much or how little detail is appropriate.

With an overresponse on each question, you may find that your discussion gets sidetracked on the unimportant issues and then you're forced to rush through key points to finish within the allotted meeting time. Shoot for the simple.

TIP 146: *Never Say, "We're the Leader . . ."*

With "We're the best . . ." or "We're number one . . . ," you invariably set high expectations that make it easy to disappoint buyers. With such braggadocio, you'll invite your customers to focus on less-than-perfect elements that shouldn't be part of the primary deal.

In fact, here's something I learned from my handyman that has stood well over time: Always overestimate costs and always underestimate results. Your customers will be pleased both when they write the check and when they see the results.

TIP 147: *Don't Talk Past Your Sales Opportunity*

Far too many sales have been lost when salespeople have rambled on, past the point buyers have been ready to buy. This often happens in team presentations during the Q&A time. That part of the presentation becomes less structured and formal and often flows into questions about implementation. At the perfect point to close, you may find that someone on your team backtracks on a technical issue and bogs down your ideal closing opportunity. All of a sudden, the key decision maker stands to say they have to rush out to another meeting. Your opportunity has now been postponed, lost, or prolonged indefinitely.

Don't keep talking. When your buyers have no further concerns, ask for their business. Then take it. And stop.

TIP 148: *Appeal to Emotions*

You've heard it said often that people buy on emotions and justify with business reasons. We do the same with marriage, voting, housing, and vacations. Long gone are the days when parents arranged the marriage of their children while they were still preschoolers. We meet, fall in love, and marry. Then we consider net worth, medical history, and IQ scores.

We drive through a neighborhood, find a house we love, and decide we want to buy it. *Then* we begin to gather data for why it makes sense to live there.

We have a negative gut reaction to a political candidate and his views on a pet policy or issue. *Then* we collect data about all the reasons we plan not to vote for him.

We decide we want and need a vacation. *Then* we set about a plan to save the money, take the time, and make it happen.

Businesses operate the same way. The CEO gets one too many angry letters or e-mails from a client about poor customer service. She picks up the phone and calls the director of all the customer support centers and tells her to buy customer service training for all 2,000 telephone support reps.

Another example: The executive vice president hates the current TV ad, calls the marketing director, and cancels the contract with the PR company.

Emotions often drive major buying decisions.

TIP 149: *Redefine the Meaning of a Buyer's Decision Criteria So That You Can Better Meet It*

When clients inform you that "easy access to technical experts" is an important buying criteria, you can't—and shouldn't—persuade them that that criteria is irrelevant or unimportant simply because you don't have a nearby office of local consultants to service their equipment. What you can do, though, is redefine what that criteria means.

For example, each time the client has referred to the need, they may have stated it like this: "We prefer a local organization. We don't have the technical expertise inside to do routine maintenance, so we'll need to call someone to come on-site for these tasks."

Your redefinition of the criteria: "So it's important to you to be able to access technical experts easily and quickly. We provide that access in three ways: through our telephone support that is available 24/7; through a contract with a local technician to handle the call for us; and through video or online documentation of all the routine maintenance so your staff can watch the video clip online to see our technical experts explain and demonstrate the procedures."

TIP 150: *Understand and Use Credibility Builders*

Credibility is a lot like charm. If you have to tell people you have it, you don't. Just as runners can always use more energy, sales professionals can always use extra credibility. Use the following credibility builders to increase yours:

- Your product or service performance
- Your company's reputation
- The right diagnostic questions
- Collateral literature
- Knowledge of your customer's business/industry
- Experience with the customer/industry
- Confident body language, personality, attitude, and appearance
- Sales presentations/your skills in delivery
- Testimonials from satisfied clients
- Objective authorities or experts
- References in memory to give immediately, along with the customer situation and resolution (evidence you know your customers well)
- Follow-up on promises where others have failed

TIP 151: *Be Opinionated—Tell Your Client What to Do*

Buyers like choices. They want to be in control and have the final say about how to meet their needs, but they also want to know what you think. After all, you have the experience of meeting with hundreds and maybe thousands of customers and have a wealth of knowledge about what works and what doesn't, about pitfalls and proven results.

As mentioned earlier, they feel much like you do when you go to your physician. You want the doctor to take charge, ask questions, gather the data, diagnose the problem, assess the situation, and give an opinion. Then they'll either accept or reject the opinion.

They expect you to get out in front and lead.

TIP 152: *Know the Difference between Continuing the Sales Dialogue and Advancing the Sale*

When selling to a team, determining that each meeting advances the sale can be difficult at times. You'll quickly need to discover if they're a collecting and recommending team or a decision-making team. If they have power only to collect and recommend, you'll need to coach them to sell you to the absent decision maker(s).

If all efforts to get yourself in front of the decision maker fail, you should then provide a written proposal—an excellent one.

You can talk for weeks, months, or years—and never close a business deal or cash a commission check. If that's happening to you all too often, go back and review your sales call planning and objective. Ask yourself: What is my single, targeted, specific, measurable objective that will advance this sale?

TIP 153: *Never Sacrifice the Client for the Sale*

Look out for the long-term best interest of the client—even if it means not making the immediate sale. We've had clients call us to say they'd like to license one of our training programs. Even though it would have meant immediate sales, we have sometimes advised them against that plan because they didn't have capable staff aboard to lead the sessions. In some cases, we felt their environment was too unstable to sustain the programs.

I recall a particular client situation with a large banking system, where one of our account executives received a call from an executive vice president (EVP) who had asked us to come out and talk to them about a consulting assignment. The account executive asked me to join her on the sales call to discuss the issues with the client. The EVP outlined the problems he had already identified, and said he had a considerable budget set aside. All we needed to do was agree to the plan and work out the scheduling details.

But the more the EVP elaborated on the situation, the more convinced I became that he was solving the wrong problem. Sure, we could have done the work and cashed the check. But, in the long run, the client situation would not have improved. When I told the EVP that his overview led me to believe he needed a different solution than what we could offer, he seemed shocked, then amazed, and then appreciative.

He ended the meeting by asking me to tell him everything we did, insisting that he wanted to find a way to work with us on some other project.

Giving up an immediate sale is never easy. Those who've made a career of selling, however, will insist that's the only way to build your client base for the long haul.

TIP 154: *Provide Periodic Management Reviews, Updates, and Reports—Even Before You've Closed the Sale*

Some salespeople shun these activities whenever possible, considering them one more time waster that cuts into their "real" selling time and eats up their profit. But think again. Consider their potential even before you've closed a sale—during the information-gathering, organizational-study phase in preparation for a large project involving a massive proposal.

Granted, such meetings and documents take time, but the benefits can be enormous. Such update meetings put you in front of the decision makers, bring multiple layers and functions together to cross-sell them on a complex offering, provide occasion to introduce others on your team, shape and increase perception of your value, position you as a strategic partner, and provide you with feedback about any negative perceptions buyers may have while there's still time for corrective action.

3

PLANNING PRESENTATIONS OF YOUR PRODUCTS AND SERVICES

"**W**ell, good morning. We appreciate the opportunity to meet with you today. My name is Simon Shultz, business development manager for InTuitWorld, and I'd like to start by introducing the rest of my team to you.

"Starting from my left is Angela Hospitch, systems engineer for the TZ500. Next is Saynar Beneviden, project manager for several current client projects, and then Nancy Lauterbach, our COO. They're here to help me answer any specific questions you have today.

"Now, with the introductions out of the way, what I'd like to do first is to tell you a little about who we are and what we do. . . . "

Another day, another proposal, another supplier, another presenter. If the parade has been going on for a couple of days—or even a few hours—you can understand buyer weariness in listening to presenter after presenter, following the same plan: "Good morning. My name is John or Joanna. My team is Tom, Dick, Harriett, Lucinda, and Lupe, and we're here to talk to you about X."

Although you may have never had a client or prospect say "I'm bored" to you directly, you may have sensed the frustration. What can you do different to make your presentation stand out from the crowd of competitors clamoring for the same business? This chapter will focus on suggestions dealing with the finer points of sales presentations.

For a complete guide on making sales presentations, see my earlier book *Speak with Confidence* (McGraw-Hill, 2003), which focuses on organizing and delivering your presentation in great detail—497 tips, in fact!

DETERMINING THE APPROPRIATE STRUCTURE

TIP 155: *Structure a Formal Presentation of Your Offering in The MADE Format®*

Don't be tempted to "tell all" in your presentation. Instead, focus on the key issues of interest to your prospect and how you differ from your competitors. Use The MADE Format for "positioning" presentations:

- *M = Message.* Summarize the results you can deliver to the buyer—how your product/service uniquely meets the buyer's need.
- *A = Action.* Recommend next steps or actions (next steps in the buying process or implementation plan).
- *D = Details.* Who? How? Where? Why? When? How much?
- *E = Evidence.* Provide any leave-behinds for later reference.

This represents the basic structure for any business presentation to any high-level executive—and especially to a buyer with a short attention span.

TIP 156: *Use a Positioning Structure Rather Than a Pitch*

Canned and formula presentations primarily make a product pitch. That is, they "tell all" about your organization and summarize one or a few key products or services (or product or service lines).

A positioning presentation, on the other hand, focuses on how your organization and your product or service *differs* from others—how it uniquely meets the buyer's needs or situation. It focuses on targeted areas of interest where your unique core strengths meet buyer criteria, and compares those strengths to alternatives.

Unless you present the same product or service to the same prospect base with the same needs, it is best to use the positioning structure for your presentations.

TIP 157: *Make a Conscious Decision about Whether to Present All Options or Only One*

When you're courting several buyers with differing viewpoints, it's natural to think that the more general you can make your presentation and recommendations, the more "hooks" you can create for the bickering buyers to latch on to. In that effort, you tend to explain your recommendations first one way and then another. You use this analogy and that. You think maybe this and maybe that would be part of the final offering. Often, the intention with the elaboration is mentioning something that will appeal to everybody.

A broad recommendation, however, usually has the opposite effect: Everybody hears something that they disagree with. As a result, you wind up spending more time dealing with the minor details and "what you didn't mean to imply" than you do with the general thrust of the proposed offering.

The group has the sense that your proposal has been thrashed to death, when in reality only the chaff around it has been discarded. Instead, make your proposal succinct, offering only one, specific way. Let it stand there in all its glory until your buyer's questions force you to add details.

TIP 158: *Analyze the Various Stages of the Customer's Mind-Set to Determine at What Point to Start Your Presentation*

When presenting to a single buyer, address the buyer's biggest needs first, as your highest priority. Next sort through the plethora of information to select what details to focus on in your discussion, based on your analysis and answers to these key questions: What does your buyer absolutely HAVE to know to decide? What do they already know about the product, service, and solution? What outcome do you want? What other bids have been considered and rejected?

When presenting to a committee or a group of buyers, let your client contact or sponsor summarize the problem and the cost of the problem before you present your solution. This will set the mood for accepting your solution and positioning its value. Watch the audience to determine your contact's credibility with the audience. Focusing on the consequence of the problem is almost always more important than focusing on value as a motivator for the group's decision.

UNDERSTANDING THE PRINCIPLES OF PERSUASION

TIP 159: *Influence, Don't Just Inform*

One of the biggest hindrances to selling success is being informative rather than persuasive. Information overwhelms us. Your role as a salesperson is to make the available information actionable for your buyers. To do that, you'll need to use all *Five Prongs of Persuasion:*

1. *Word choice.* Positive, specific, precise words
2. *Rhetoric.* Powerful phrasing and graceful grammar that pack a powerful punch on a buyer's memory
3. *Emotion.* Feelings of either pleasure, fear, safety, discomfort, pride, acceptance, rejection, or prestige
4. *Logic.* Reasoning and conclusions drawn from facts, information, opinions, or ideas
5. *Trustworthiness.* Trust in an individual's or organization's principles, values, and integrity

To persuade, you need to know and use the best words, to establish your own and your organization's credibility, and to identify the best strategies with each buyer—whether that be primarily an appeal to emotion or an appeal to logic, or a combination of both.

TIP 160: *Act against Your Own Self-Interest*

Nothing underscores your determination to do what's right for the buyer more than making them aware of decisions made in their best interest. You may routinely do that anyway, but buyers need to know when you do that because it builds trust for larger issues. For example, if you think an extended warranty doesn't make sense for a particular customer, instead of not bringing it up at all, let the buyer know a warranty is available but that you recommend against it.

Let's say the buyer is selecting tiling for break rooms and restroom facilities throughout their buildings and has already made it known that they prefer "the best" in everything. The color choices are black and beige, with a surcharge of 10 percent for the black. Assuming the most expensive is "the best," the buyer selects black. Yet, you know that customers have complained that black shows scratches more readily and requires more care than the lighter color. You may pass along this information and suggest that the beige might make a better choice in the buyer's high-traffic areas.

Such candid advice leads to increased trust—but only if your buyer understands that you're making such decisions to pass on such information at your own expense. Subtly, of course.

TIP 161: *Use the "Experience" Factor*

Buyers can argue about your facts, data, surveys, and research. They can disagree that your product or services outshine the competition. They can doubt that your offering will resolve their problem.

But no one can dispute your experience when you state an opinion or respond to a question during your presentation. For example, your buyer asks: "I think customizing the assessment is a waste of time. Why are you thinking we need a customized version added to our intranet before we roll this out to our own customers?" You respond: "That has to be your final decision, of course. It will delay the project approximately two months. In my experience in handling these projects for more than 70 clients during the past two years, I can recall only two clients who skipped that phase, and both regretted the decision because their own employees proved to be a great cross-section of the population to test user acceptance. I offer that experience for your consideration."

Your experience is *your* experience. It can be accepted or rejected, but it's still your experience and irrefutable as such.

TIP 162: *Use Success Stories*

Anecdotes and success stories—whether about other client organizations or collected from interviews in the buyer's organization—add powerful finishing touches to capture a buyer's attention. Buyers are often persuaded by success stories of other organizations in similar situations as theirs or of respected leaders in other industries.

Such stories reach a buyer's emotion. In fact, prospects often remember your stories more than your facts. In many, if not most, cases, buying decisions are made based on both emotion and logic.

There also are pitfalls in using stories. Always consider carefully any details you share in success stories. Even without mentioning names, your buyer may be able to deduce information about a competitor. Not only will you have a conflict of interest and an ethical dilemma on your hands, you may unknowingly frighten the buyer away from dealing with you.

TIP 163: *Tell Failure Stories*

There is power in telling case histories about clients who did not have stellar success with your product or service—if the reason for their lack of success was due to their own decision making, not your product or service. It underscores what other customers did wrong (for example, waiting too long to buy, not using your design team to install and customize their product, not buying a warranty) and helps the current prospect not repeat the mistake. Telling about failures of other product users adds credibility to your success stories.

One caution: Don't use names with the failure stories, because prospects may fear you'll tell others of their own mistakes later if they buy.

TIP 164: *Collect Evidence and Present Proof—But Don't Expect It to Clinch the Deal*

Presenting proof to your prospects makes a powerful presentation—but proof alone rarely makes a sale. Many a sales professional has wasted enormous time gathering proof—such as work samples—only to discover that a prospect wouldn't agree that these things proved anything. Always agree on what the buyer will accept as proof.

Next, verify that your buyer considers such proof *meaningful*. For example, you may prove that your engine is faster than any on the market, but if your prospect values low-cost maintenance more than speed, your proof will be "beside the point."

If both you and your prospect agree to a specific test, verify who will pay for it. If you and your organization cover the cost, document that your buyer is prepared to buy once the testing is complete. In my early days of supervising account executives, I remember—unfavorably—one of our star performers coming in to propose to me that we do a "teach off" for a very large client with several thousand people to be trained in one of our interpersonal skills programs. Located across the country, the client proposed that we fly in our instructors to conduct a "pilot" program for them to evaluate and compare to their in-house course as well as to other competitors' courses. We did—at considerable inconvenience on a very short timetable. The test scores were exceptional.

We won. But we also lost—the client never made a buying decision at all. As it turns out, they had no budget—the ambitious and clever manager who set up the "teach off" received training for several groups of people at rock-bottom rates and only "hoped to have some money sometime in the future." I learned my lesson very early on to get the commitment before the test.

Next, document your proof in writing so others can verify it. It's always advisable to capture your data and publish it in an article or white paper (see Tip 438), for example, so that it passes scrutiny of all concerned.

Also, be sure to calculate the minimum gain needed to justify the investment. Ask your client specifically: "What percentage of decrease in customer complaints would make this solution worthwhile for you?" It's far easier to get a team of buyers to agree on *minimum* projections on savings than on *maximums*.

Finally, don't build your whole presentation around your proof, counting on it as "the sure thing." People buy for any number of reasons, and logical proof is only one of them.

TIP 165: *Prefer Understatement to Overstatement*

After my teenage son came home from his first summer job interview as a grocery stocker, I asked how it went. "I don't know," he said. "They gave me one of those honesty tests, where they asked if I'd ever cheated on an exam, if I'd ever stolen money from my parents, if I'd ever shoplifted—things like that." He paused, looked a little concerned, then added, "I was answering no to all those things and then I got a little worried that maybe I wouldn't get the job—that I sounded too good to be true."

He did get the job, but it was an astute observation about human nature.

It's always more effective to let your prospect "add to" what you've promised rather than "discount it" because it seems too good to be believable. Present the range of results you have achieved and can document. Generally, it is better to promise only the minimum gains. Otherwise, you set up your client to be disappointed. If the minimum gains are worthwhile to them, maximum gains will be the "extra" that makes them long-term fans.

TIP 166: *Source All Testimonials*

Names always lend credibility to testimonials—whether you're citing them orally in your presentation, using them in a brochure, or providing them in a letter or e-mail. Always be sure you have permission from the referenced client, and let the prospect know that you have such permission. Using a client name—even in a success story—can be trouble if the buyer thinks you are revealing confidential information. They may shy away from dealing with you for fear that you'll reveal proprietary information about their own organization.

TIP 167: *Know When to Use Exact Numbers and When to Round Them*

Exact numbers are more credible because they more easily can be verified and either confirmed or discounted. Rounded numbers, on the other hand, are easier to remember. Provide specific numbers the first time you cite results or outcomes, and then summarize with rounded numbers on repeat mention of the data.

TIP 168: *Make Statistics and Facts Experiential*

People digest numbers with great difficulty. Yes, pie charts and bar graphs help. But if you can go beyond that, do so. For example, randomly survey your committee of buyers by asking them to raise their hands in response to a few questions; then equate those findings to the random survey you did previously of their entire organization. Are they typical of the rest of the employee population? How so?

Supporting statistics lend credibility to what you say. Be sure, however, to do all you can to help your buyers digest them.

TIP 169: *Never Shy Away from the Underdog Positioning*

Some people have a profound penchant for rooting for the underdog. Consider acknowledging that you're the lesser-known brand and supplier, and focus on the effort you intend to expend for the client because of that one-down situation. Avis has done very well with the underdog status as their brand.

TIP 170: *Use the Jelly Principle*

Presenting bad news to clients or prospects is never easy—particularly, when you're in the middle of trying to close a sale.

Examples of bad news: "We've compared your data with best practices in the industry, and you're way below standard." "You can't buy *anybody's* widget for that budget!" "The guarantee is far less than you expect—and ours is the strongest in the industry."

Think back to your childhood—when a parent gave you bad-tasting medicine camouflaged in another food you liked, such as jelly. The same principle comes in handy with bitter messages. You may have to wrap negative messages in a more pleasing idea or get them across in more subtle ways.

TIP 171: *Ask for a Suspension of Judgment*

When you're involved in a complex sale with multiple buyers and you know that some of your buyers are going to be dead set against what you have to say—or at least heavily biased toward other options—admit that situation. Not bluntly, of course, but diplomatically. Chances are good—with such an open but subtle acknowledgment of competition and other alternatives—that your buyers will give you a fair hearing, and that's all you need.

TIP 172: *Create a Customized "To-Do"*

Maybe it's time to make a big "to-do" about your buyer! Make your prospects feel special by creating a unique experience to earn their attention and business. Here are some examples:

- Host a trade-show hospitality suite
- Fly them to your site for a tour
- Send them a book on their personal interest
- Mail a unique gift or gadget related to your offering
- Create an educational seminar about industry trends or for personal growth
- Introduce them to a potential new customer or partner for *their own* benefit

- Create a "summit" to bring their key players together for discussion
- Set up a unique demonstration of your product

These are just a few ideas for events, but they may tweak your recall of others you've created, seen colleagues use, or experienced yourself as a buyer. Look at the success record of business won that you can track to such events. If it seems profitable, consider this strategy again for key prospects on big opportunities.

TIP 173: *"Review" Your Proposal with a Buyer Before You "Present" It*

Politicians make a habit of leaking their plans to the press to see what public reaction is before they etch policies in stone. Ad agencies test their marketing campaigns in small markets before a full-scale roll out of the commercial or ad. Direct-mailers test mailing lists with 5,000 names before mailing to a million households.

You'll do well to follow the same principle with your prospects. Jot down the key provisions of your offering or written proposal and set an appointment to review these "talking" points with your buyer before you officially "present" the offering. Get reactions. Read their body language. Ask: "Does this sound feasible with your XYZ policies?" "How will this work with the deadlines Joe Smoe expressed?" "Is this what you had in mind?" "Have I covered all your key issues?"

When you're sure you have addressed all the important criteria with the appropriate emphasis, then redraft your proposal and plan your "official" presentation.

TIP 174: *Plant Questions You'd Like Competitors to Address*

As you present your solutions, subtly bring up issues that should raise red flags in your buyers' minds about the capabilities of your competitors. You won't challenge or attack competitors specifically; however, in your key areas of strength, you will suggest issues that, if not handled well, might create pitfalls and resulting fear in the minds of your buyers. Simply by raising these issues, you will suggest to your buyers that they should ask your competitors about these same concerns.

TIP 175: *Never Just "Walk Through" Your Proposal—Give a Guided Tour*

Your buyers will beat you to the end every time. Buyers follow their own route, which is usually not the one you'd prefer. While you're still on page two, your buyers will be on page eight, checking out the pricing section. You have absolutely no control of what your buyers hear or pay attention to while you talk. In fact, your proposal will compete with you for attention.

Instead, carefully select which parts of your proposal to present orally. Then if you want to refer your buyers to a specific page, do so—*after* you make your key point about that page.

TIP 176: *Lead Buyers to "Interact" with Your Written Proposal*

A primary purpose for written proposals is for preview or review. Imagine your buyers in a complex sales situation with proposals from four competitors. The proposal review team, seated around a conference table, is discussing the oral presentations heard a week earlier. As they skim the accompanying proposals, where will their eyes fall? Correct—everywhere they've marked something on the page or written a note in the margin.

During your oral presentation, your job will be to ask buyers to highlight key points and make notes in the margin for later recall. Plan how you'll do that—questions you'll raise, data that surfaces during your proposal discussion, or questions they ask during the Q&A time following your formal presentation.

TIP 177: *Be the Catalyst to Bring the Right People into the Room*

Getting all the right people—from your organization and the buyer's organization—in the same room can be a difficult task. Aside from the difficulty, keep in mind that this strategy is not without its pitfalls: Introducing new people and opinions into the situation midstream may create political problems. You may unknowingly create tension between conflicting personalities. When you involve more people in the buyer's decision-making process, it may, on occasion, lengthen the sales cycle in and of itself. Thus, your role as facilitator of any such meeting or presentation will also require extra skill.

If you can pull off this feat of getting all the kingpins together, you'll have two key advantages:

1. Bringing in your own senior executives will elevate the importance of the decision.
2. Getting all the players together in one presentation can shorten the sales cycle dramatically.

TIP 178: *Know When to Sit and When to Stand*

Stand if you want to convey authority and underscore the importance of an issue. When you "rise to the occasion," the buyers and your own sales team generally settle back and let you have the floor. The group dynamics change from an informal team discussion to a formal presentation. A formal presentation conveys three things: "I have an opinion already on this issue and a formal recommendation of product or services." "I am well prepared with supporting details." "This meeting is bigger and more important than the routine interactions we've had to this point."

From your physically-elevated position, your words take on more authority; the group is likely to grant you control of the meeting, even if only temporarily. As a result of these dynamics, you probably will get less feedback on your overview and proposal. Those who support you will withhold their comments, thinking that you obviously sound authoritative and need no help in garnering others' opinions. Those who disagree may hate to buck authority before an audience; they often save their negative comments for the hallways.

You sometimes can "have it both ways" by presenting your proposal standing up and then taking a seat for the follow-up discussion.

The best delivery style of all, of course, is to be able to move easily back and forth between an authoritative and confident presentation of your recommendations and a facilitation style of Q&A as details and issues arise.

TIP 179: *Consider Your Demeanor—Don't Confuse Boring for Sincere*

Create flair and drama as you present a new idea, recommendation, product, or service to your prospect. Having wanted to shed the huckster image of 40 or 50 years ago, some sales professionals have gone to the other extreme and removed all animation, inflection, and energy from their delivery style in an effort to come across as more "sincere."

Instead of sincere, the result has been lackluster and boring.

If you're not passionate about your proposal, neither will your buyers be. Never confuse genuine enthusiasm for lack of professionalism. If you want to see the passion and power to move a world to action, watch the delivery styles of world leaders and listen to their vocal variety.

Don't let a passionless demeanor destroy your prospect's confidence in your offering.

TIP 180: *Determine If the Prospect Wants to Pursue or Be Pursued*

Conventional wisdom holds that prospects don't want to "be sold"—they prefer to buy. Don't take that to mean that's the case with *all* prospects. As in love and romance, some prospects actually enjoy the pursuit stage. They especially want to know that you don't take their repeat business for granted. Therefore, they begin to talk about "considering all options" when it comes time to renew contracts. Pay attention to such signals and language to know which mind-set your prospect has—to pursue or be pursued—and get in lockstep with that expectation.

SELECTING MEMORABLE, POWERFUL LANGUAGE

TIP 181: *Eliminate Limp Language*

Limp language includes hedgers, tag questions, disclaimers, intensifiers, and phony, canned phrasing such as the following:

- *Canned/Formal/Phony.* "Manufacturing-process teams have pioneered the use of high-speed machining and automated fiber placement for producing one-piece metallic and composite structures that are stronger and lighter than multipiece structures."
- *Intensifiers.* "*much, much* lower" "*so very* exciting" "*highly* reliable"
- *Hedging.* "We'll try to do everything possible." "We'll make every attempt to . . ."
- *Tag questions.* "Don't you think?" "Wouldn't you agree?" "Haven't I?"
- *Disclaimers and qualifiers.* "subject to change without notice" "delivery schedules may vary, depending on season of the year" "under normal business conditions" "within the range of customary expenses"

Such limp language loses sales.

TIP 182: *Use Triads to Focus on Core Points*

Triads are groupings of threes: three words, three phrases, or three short sentences—often that rhyme, such as the following:

- "It's quick, safe, and reliable."
- "It's a turnkey option: Delivered. Installed. Trained."
- "When you think of our consulting group, think of three things: Innovation. Motivation. Integration."

TIP 183: *Use Alliteration to Tease the Ear*

Alliteration refers to words that start with the same sound or rhyme in other ways, often triads.

- "We want to help you reach your own customers. Our goal will be to help you *plan, promote, and produce.*"
- "Our contracts are *clear, complete, and concise.*"
- "*Assess* your needs. *Access* your database. *Allocate* your resources. *Apply* our technology."

TIP 184: *Use Analogies and Metaphors for Quick Insight*

Metaphors and analogies create powerful pictures. One metaphor can convey a lifetime of experience or a head full of logic. In one of my client workshops, a sales rep used an analogy comparing his software package to socks. Black dress socks worn every day to the office represented data files needed daily. These dress socks would go in the top drawer for easy access just like data files retrieved often must be easy to access. White athletic socks worn for exercising only on the weekends represented data files that were used monthly or quarterly. These white socks would be stored in the middle bureau drawer for limited access just like data files needed occasionally but not daily. The green plaid socks worn only when Aunt Martha came to visit represented the data files needed only once a year. These plaid socks would be stored in the bottom bureau drawer for infrequent access just like inactive files that may never be needed again. His audience immediately understood the concept behind his software package—storage of data as it relates to retrieval time.

We occasionally explain to customers the various fee arrangements of our licensing of intellectual properties with this analogy: "As you determine which is the best fee arrangement for your organization, consider it a mortgage. You can pay for a house with all cash up front, or you can pay for it over time with interest. The last arrangement will cost you more over time, but you have your money free to use for other things as you go along." Customers understand the concept: they can make an outright purchase or they can take out a mortgage. Metaphors clarify what would take hours to explain in detail.

Analogies have the same effect as eyeglasses: You understand something new by looking through familiar lenses.

Analogies do not need to be compared in several ways to be effective. In fact, two things may be alike only in one respect, and that one way may be your key comparison point. Also pay attention to length. The longer the illustration or analogy, the better the points must be to keep the buyer's attention. Brief is better—with analogies, illustrations, humor, or anecdotes of almost any kind in a sales situation.

Of course, analogies never *prove* anything; they only clarify or illustrate.

TIP 185: *Look for an Antithesis for a Provocative Comparison*

Antitheses are opposites juxtaposed—placed side by side for comparison. Example: "The real question is not, Can you afford this equipment; I think the real question is, Can you afford the downtime without it?"

TIP 186: *Capture Your Message in Slogans and Themes*

Attorneys know that if they can think of a powerful phrase for the jurors to take into the juror room, that single phrase may win their client freedom. According to legal analysts, Johnny Cochran's "If it doesn't fit, you must acquit" won O.J. Simpson's freedom in what was dubbed "the trial of the century."

Politicians understand that if they can capsule their platform in a three- to ten-word slogan, voters will remember it when they walk into the voting booth. Movie producers know that a great title can draw a crowd to a mediocre movie.

CEOs and marketing mavens understand that a clever new advertising slogan can make an old product fly off the shelves.

Use a slogan in your oral presentation, on your visuals, in your written proposal, and in your follow-up discussions as you advance the sale through implementation.

4

GAINING COMMITMENT
AND CLOSING

Sales language and thinking have come full circle. That's as it should be and has to be because our selling environment and clients continue to change. Fifty years ago, master sales professionals talked about the importance of grabbing attention, creating interest, overcoming objections, and using surefire closing techniques. Soon after, sales masters preached the consultative approach and relationship selling. They insisted that if you did things correctly, there would be no "objections" and no need to "close," but to simply "gain commitment" to move ahead and finish the paperwork in the completed sales process.

A few years later, master sales professionals came along who said, "Well, it all depends." They began to categorize sales by size. Closing techniques may work well with small-ticket, transactional sales, but closing techniques also may work with large-ticket sales because even those sales are now often transactional. Recent buyers have educated themselves on the Internet and want to close the sale quickly over the phone. In large-ticket situations with *multiple* buyers, though, a quick close may not even be desirable—lingering through the sales cycle may open additional opportunities.

Today, sales masters know that you can "close" a sale (if you mean "gain commitment," such as have a buyer set up a purchase order or tell the troops that you're the preferred supplier for product X) and *still* not have the buyer implement the sale.

Definitely, you do need to close sales. They don't close themselves. But closing is a process, not a single event that happens before you walk out the door or hang up the phone. (Remember how the old line, "always be closing," was eliminated from our vocabulary in the 1980s because it reeked of high-pressure tactics? Maybe we need to bring it back—but with a very different meaning today.)

Keeping that difference in mind—closing as an event versus as a process—will change everything you do in the sales cycle.

GENERAL GUIDELINES: RESPONDING TO CONCERNS

TIP 187: *Distinguish between Concerns, Conditions, and Excuses*

A condition is a legitimate reason the prospect cannot buy, something over which they have no control or influence. For example, the prospect has no authority or no money, or the company's being bought out and all purchases are frozen.

An objection is a legitimate concern raised about a product or service about which the prospect is still undecided. It may be a real unresolved concern or a mishandled sales call or failure to show value or create awareness of a need. An excuse, on the other hand, is a comment offered to delay or avoid having to say no.

So what can you do when you're facing each situation? Respond to a prospect's concerns. Either help the buyer change a condition, or walk away. Avoid excuses.

TIP 188: *Don't Respond Too Quickly to Concerns*

With unduly quick responses, you'll sound like the stereotypically fast-talking salesperson. Buyers may feel minimized, invalidated, pressured, or intimidated.

TIP 189: *Ask for Elaboration on a Concern before Responding*

Without elaboration, you'll find it difficult to determine if a comment is a condition, concern, or excuse (see Tip 187). Here are example probes that help you get at the heart of a buyer's comment: "How do you mean?" "Can you elaborate on that?" "What exactly will you be comparing us to in that regard?" "Can you clarify your criteria on that issue, please?" "How important is that issue to you—I didn't hear that mentioned earlier?" "Is this something that's relatively important to you?"
Assumptions can be dangerous.

TIP 190: *Don't "Overanswer" in Response to a Concern*

Responses that are too lengthy elevate the importance of the concern and signal to buyers that the negative issue does indeed warrant focus. Answer clearly and directly, and then move on.

TIP 191: *Avoid Asking "Does This Answer Your Concern?"*

If you continue to receive questions from a buyer on a matter of concern, by all means, continue to elaborate and clarify. Asking "Does this answer your concern?" as a routine, however, has two negative effects: 1) Some prospects fear that a yes commits them to make a "buy" decision, and 2) when prospects respond with a no, you're in a position to confront and argue with them that you have, indeed, answered their concern.

Generally, it is best to clarify and assess for yourself whether the concern seems to be allayed rather than to ask for verbal assurance, which is often seen as manipulative.

TIP 192: *Phrase Responses to Objections as "Can You Elaborate?" Instead of "What Do You Mean?"*

"What do you mean?" can sound threatening and defensive and may shut buyers down before they voice the hidden concerns that will keep them from buying. The open-ended "Can you elaborate?" or "How do you mean?" invites more explanation and clarification to almost any buyer comment. (Yes, I know, the Grammar Grinch will tell you "Can you elaborate?" means "Are you able?" But your prospect will understand and appreciate your welcoming phrasing.)

TIP 193: *Reverse Buyer Concerns to "Reason to Change" Statements*

For example, let's say your buyer says to you: "I'm rocking along okay with the equipment I have—no problems now. It should last me another two to three years." The buyer is concerned that they'll be making an unnecessary purchase. You'll then need to explain the value in replacing the older equipment with better equipment sooner—the value in increased efficiency from faster production or decreased maintenance or operation costs.

Your response: "I understand that the equipment you have now has served you well and in fact is still in good condition. So you're going to *need a logical reason* to trade it in at this point. I think I can give you a couple of reasons that a trade-in would actually mean money in your pocket over the next three years. One reason to consider a trade now is that. . . ."

TIP 194: *Never Repeat Negative Words in the Concern from a Buyer*

Politicians, sports celebrities, CEOs, and movie stars learn in Media Training 101 never to repeat negative words in response to a reporter's question. Why? A negative phrase always trumps a positive phrase; it's what gets hammered home in the minds of viewers. Example:

The reporter asks: "Did you cheat on your income taxes?"

Interviewee: "Of course, I didn't cheat on my taxes. What—do you think I'm crazy enough to cheat on my taxes? Every law agency in the country—federal, state, local—would be after me. I hate tax cheats myself. I've never cheated on my taxes, and I don't intend to start cheating on my taxes at this stage in my life. If all my opponent can come up with is that I cheat on my taxes, they don't have a platform."

So what do you remember? "Cheating on taxes," right?

Repetition of negative concerns has the same effect in a sales situation. Respond by rephrasing the concern, minus the negative words.

Example of buyer's concern: "The up-front cost for the add-ons just seems *way too high.*"

Weak response: "Actually, the up-front charge is standard in the industry. The charge may seem high, but really it just covers the cost of customizing."

Better response by recasting: "The reason we ask for a *50 percent deposit* up front to cover the *customizing* is because the packaging cannot be resold after we've added your logo to each unit. The deposit is standard in the industry."

TIP 195: *Never Contradict and Become Confrontational*

If you win, you lose. Don't minimize issues buyers mention by making them feel ridiculous or stupid. Instead, acknowledge the legitimacy of the feeling or the concern. Respond with a brief, positive explanation, and then move on.

Never badger with insulting comments such as: "Don't you want to save money?" "Aren't you interested in improving your operations?" "Don't you care about staying up to date in your field?" Such comments deserve a slammed door or a disconnected line.

CONCERNS ABOUT PRICING

TIP 196: *Convince Yourself That Your Pricing Is Appropriate*

A cardinal communication principle is that we tend to see and hear what we expect to see and hear. Many pricing objections grow from the seed planted in the mind of the salesperson. They don't truly understand the value of their own products and, therefore, they don't state them with conviction. Almost before the buyer bats an eye, they're offering concessions or suggesting ways to "save money" on a "less expensive" solution or plan. Buyers will pick up these clues and quickly follow your lead.

Investigate your own pricing structure and the value you can deliver to the buyer. State your price with pride and confidence.

TIP 197: *Isolate the Multiple Meanings of "Your Price Is Too High" Before You Respond*

If you go to your doctor and complain of pain, the doctor's first question to you will be, "Where does it hurt?" Only when the doctor knows the symptoms or location of the pain can they begin to address the matter.

The same follows in a sales situation. If you shoot from the hip in your response, you have a one-in-nine chance of addressing the concern appropriately. The prospect may mean any of these things with such a comment:

- "I don't understand the value. It doesn't seem worth the cost."
- "Your price is over my budget or authorization limit."
- "Your price is more than I paid last time."
- "Your price is more than my colleague/friend said it should cost."
- "Your price is more than I hoped to pay—I had no idea it would cost that much."
- "The economy is bad, and my business has been slow."
- "I'm not sure I need it that much."
- "Your price is 1 percent higher than your competitor's."
- "Your price is okay—but that excuse is as good as any when I have a political hot potato that I can't tell you about."

Probe to discover the meaning of the comment so you can address the issue effectively and lead the buyer to reset expectations.

Example probes: "I understand that everybody these days is concerned about price. When you say 'expensive,' what exactly are you comparing the price to?" "Are you familiar with the maintenance support and guarantees this price includes?" "What did you have budgeted per unit on your last annual contract?" "Has each division been paying for these items at their local hardware stores in small neighbor cities around the country? Have you included their time in ordering and processing in that cost?"

TIP 198: *Stress Value*

Mention quality of workmanship, controlled maintenance, availability of technical support, access to superior expertise, leading-edge styling, predictable reliability, continuous innovation, market research as the basis for features and updates, frequent deliveries, guarantees, replacement policies, convenience, location, buyer education and consultation, quick implementation, environmentally responsible, and safety track record.

TIP 199: *Focus on the Total Cost of Ownership*

Help your buyer understand the difference between price and the total cost of ownership, either by asking a clarifying question or sharing "failure stories" of prospects who later returned to buy from you.

Example: Recently, we decided to remodel our patio bathroom so we could update with the latest colors to put our house on the market. A general contractor gave us a bid of $12,500 to redo the room with new fixtures, wallpaper, lighting, and a mirror. Too high, we decided, after hearing that our friends had contracted directly with several workers and had done their own remodeling work for much less.

So we shopped for the bathroom fixtures, wallpaper, lighting, faucet set, and mirror ourselves—and the price on all these items was less than $8,000. So far, so good.

The first plumber we hired bolted the pedestal lavatory to the wall crooked and dropped and cracked the toilet base. But he installed it and billed us without pointing out the crack, hoping we wouldn't notice his glued repair until much later. We had to have another plumber redo the crooked lavatory job and replace the leaking toilet.

We spent only three Saturdays shopping for an odd-shaped mirror to fit the space. Then the faucets, which had already been installed, didn't match the mirror. So we had to buy a third faucet unit and again pay the plumber to replace it after the crooked pedestal sink was reinstalled.

The wallpaper hanger was a real bargain. She did the job for $291, plus cost of the designer paper, which began to come apart at the seams about two weeks after she hung it. She had not taken the time to remove all the old paper. We had to pay a second wallpaper hanger to repair the first job.

Total cost of "owning" the remodeled patio bathroom? Don't ask.

When your own buyers express concern about price and compare it to competitors' products or services, probe or share an illustration to help them differentiate between your up-front *price* versus the lifetime *cost* of ownership.

TIP 200: *Offer a Variety of Financing Options*

Provide options such as credit plans, installment payments, or discounts based on volume or multiyear contracts.

TIP 201: *Ask Questions That Lead to Comparisons of Value and Price*

When your buyers start to compare your price to that of competitors, probe gently with questions that focus on the total value. Examples: "Did you notice if the equipment had this same durable steel casing around the engine?" "Did the other pricing arrangements include 24/7 technical support at no additional cost?" "Were you aware that our pricing includes complimentary consultations with our staff for the first 120 days after you install the system? That's very helpful for most first-time users."

TIP 202: *"Reinvent" Your Price Comparisons*

A dozen red roses can be compared to a dozen red roses, right? Wrong. Not if you sell your red roses in a decorative pot and now call it a rose basket. A hotel room can be compared to a hotel room—unless your hotel room includes a suite, a breakfast, and cocktail hors d'oeuvres and drinks.

A week's rental for a resort condo can be compared to a week's rental for a resort condo—unless your resort condo is on a cruise ship moving from holiday paradise to holiday paradise. Tuition costs for certification can be compared to tuition costs for certification—unless your graduates are guaranteed job placement upon graduating.

You get the picture. Can you repackage your offering so that it sits in a category all its own?

TIP 203: *Hang a Price Tag on Each Benefit*

Lead buyers to calculate the price tag, benefit by benefit. For example, let's say you sell office supplies to large corporations and the buyers consider your price too high because they're comparing the price of your office supplies delivered to their office stock room with the price of what they can buy the items for at a local office supply retail store.

You might literally write down the costs this way:

	Our Service	Local Retailer
Three dozen widgets	$38.97	$32.97
Delivered vs. pick up	0	?
Ordering time for you	0	?
Monitoring supplies so you don't run out and have downtime	0	?
Discount on bulk orders	5%	0

Ask for their input to replace your question marks in the chart. Whether your buyers decide on an exact amount is beside the point. Your goal is to have them evaluate each benefit they're buying.

TIP 204: *State the Prorated Cost*

A lump sum can sound staggering. Does it make sense to break down your price so that your buyers can think of the investment per X hours, days, years, groups, or number of users?

For example, on a consulting project, the fee might sound exorbitant—until you phrase it like this: "Actually, that price breaks down to about $60 per hour for our analysts—a very reasonable rate for their experience level." If you are pricing access charges to a specific service, you might quote the price as "only $X per user per month."

TIP 205: *Show Industry Data about Pricing or Value*

Some customers just don't have a clue. That is, they honestly don't know what to expect to pay for the product or service they need, and neither do they understand the true value of how it can improve their operations. As an excellent sales professional, you will have probably presented such benefits earlier in the sales discussions, but your buyer may have taken your statements at face value because there was no dollar sign on the other side of the scale.

After price surfaces, your explanation about such benefits may need more authoritative sources to support them. Rather than grabbing for your charts with a "see there" tone and attitude, ask "permission" to show your buyer recent industry studies that will support the value of your product or service—reduced overhead costs, less downtime, fewer repairs, safer operations, quicker processing, and so forth.

TIP 206: *Stir Only the Hot Sauce—Not the Whole Enchilada*

At the point of closing, you already will have discussed the value of various benefits of your product or service. There's no need to justify the entire price if the buyer's hesitancy is based only on comparison to competing products or services. Instead, you simply need to justify the *difference*—what does the buyer get for the extra $22 on the price tag? Don't go back through the pricing on the whole enchilada—that will only stir up the hot sauce. Justify only the difference in price—not the total price.

TIP 207: *Add a Premium Instead of Offering a Discount*

Consider including something as a bonus that will not reduce your profit margin but that will increase the value to your buyer: free delivery, free installation, free customization, free training, an extended warranty, access to an expert, technical support for a limited time, accessories, waived processing fees or restocking charges if necessary to return an item, or a sale price on related items.

TIP 208: *Spill Secrets, Then Ask the Buyer's Priority*

When buyers bring up the issue of pricing or begin to talk about lower competitive product or services, simply explain this fact of the marketplace: "Some buyers always prefer the best quality. Some shop for excellent service and support. Others make their decision based on the lowest up-front price. Suppliers can't offer all three. Which is your primary criteria for this decision—product quality, excellent service, lowest up-front price?"

If a buyer continues to insist that other competitors do offer all three, you may want to "spill the beans" about how other suppliers make certain offers. Do be careful, however, that you don't attack a specific competitor.

Instead, speak generically: "Some companies are able to offer huge sales and discounts on these services—for a very limited time. Generally, such promotional programs involve a cut-rate monthly fee for a short three- to six-month period and then rates go back to the normal structure. While you can save a few dollars initially, if you decide their service isn't reliable during that period, then you're out the expense of having to pay another installation charge to change your service to another supplier later."

Consider it leveling with the buyer about the realities of the marketplace.

TIP 209: *Redefine the Scope of the Project, Service, or Product*

When your buyers cannot afford your product, work on a cost-reduction plan with them. Suggest ways they can trim the cost. For example, can they do part of the data-collection and preparation process on a project? Can they use workers with less expertise? Can they schedule the project in off-peak periods? Can they assume liability issues?

With products, can you lead them to a model with fewer bells and whistles that will still meet their primary objectives? Must the product be customized? Can they take a slightly flawed model that doesn't meet your typical standards?

With services, can you lead them to reduce the typical standards? Reduce the frequency? Accept less efficiency in the process?

Any cost you save as a supplier then can be passed on to them.

TIP 210: *Stand Firm and Assure Buyers They Are Getting Your Best Price*

People sometimes ask about price simply because they're afraid they're about to be taken. This is particularly true of large corporations and affluent individuals. They fear that suppliers will quote a high price based on their obvious ability to pay. Address this concern by refusing to waiver. Assure them that you are quoting them your standard pricing arrangement.

TIP 211: *Never Accept at Face Value What Buyers Tell You about Competitor Pricing*

Buyers are like the rest of the population—they have faulty memories, they don't ask the details, they don't always notice quality distinctions, and they make apples-to-oranges comparisons.

TIP 212: *Never Emphasize Your Own Overhead or Costs as Supplier*

Buyers don't care—your costs are not their problem.

CONCERNS ABOUT PRICING— BUYERS ASKING TOO EARLY

TIP 213: *Defer Early Questions about Price*

After your buyers understand the value of what you offer and then hear the price, they'll be more likely to have the reaction, "That's a good deal." If forced to discuss price early, you'll want to balance each mention with a value.

Defer early questions from your buyer with comments such as: "I'll come to that in a moment." "You'll be happy to hear that when I get to it shortly." "I'm sure you've shopped around, and we're very competitive with the quality providers." "I plan to discuss the price in context in a few moments." "I want to make sure we have the right product first, and then we'll get to price." "That varies. But I'll nail it down for you as we get further along and I understand exactly what you want."

TIP 214: *State That You Need to Collect Information First*

Explain that you'd be guessing at the situation: "I don't want to give you a guess at this point. If you can wait until we're finished with this questionnaire and the testing, I'll have all the information I need to help me identify exactly the best matches. I prefer to be accurate from the start. Is that okay with you?"

TIP 215: *Ask What Price Range Is on the Buyer's Mind*

Probe with: "You seem concerned about price. Did you have a specific price range in mind?" If price is the buyer's major criteria, then you can direct them to the most appropriate choices more quickly than going on a fishing expedition.

But you also may lose the opportunity to provide the buyer with a better value if you limit your offering to that price category. At some point during the discussion, it's generally a good idea to show your best quality as well. Many buyers will later base their decision on quality rather than price when educated about the options. Those who stay with lowest price will still be happy with their bargain.

TIP 216: *Offer a Range of Pricing Options*

If your buyer persists in asking about price before you've had opportunity to establish value, mention a range: "We offer units from about

$7,000 to $20,000, depending on the bells and whistles and the kind of engine you need." "Our hourly fees range from $60-$320, depending on the experience of the consultants assigned to your project. We'll be able to identify who you'll need as we discuss your project in more detail."

CONCERNS ABOUT HIGHER PRIORITY TO SPEND MONEY ELSEWHERE

TIP 217: *Increase the Value of Your Solution*

Typically, you can increase the value of your solution four ways. If you're creative, you even can expand on and combine some of these ways:

1. Make the buyer aware of more benefits.
2. Make the buyer aware of more advantages that flow from each benefit.
3. Increase the number of recipients of those benefits: Can you expand the circle of those who will benefit to more departments, more divisions, or more users per group? Can the buyer extend the benefits to their own customers or suppliers?
4. Extend the length of time each benefit or advantage will last.

TIP 218: *Ask Buyers to Think Short Term*

When buyers consider priorities, they're thinking of doing either/or based on timing. If they're inclined to spend their first dollars elsewhere, then obviously they see your solution as something that can wait. Your job is to create urgency. What can they gain by doing something immediately as opposed to postponing the purchase?

TIP 219: *Ask Buyers to Think Long Term*

If your buyers are inclined to spend their first dollars elsewhere because they have labeled a pressing need "urgent," they may be focused on makeshift, shortsighted solutions, or even frivolous expenditures. They may not have considered the long-term cost of failure to solve bigger problems—needs your product or service could meet.

Your job is to direct their attention away from the pressing "urgency" to the important. Force them to think about the long-term effects of such decisions. What will they lose by postponing their purchase?

CONCERNS ABOUT A BAD PAST EXPERIENCE

TIP 220: *Be Empathetic*

Saying "I'm sorry" doesn't equate to liability. You can accept responsibility for a situation, outcome, hassle, or frustration without ever admitting fault. The buyer knows that you personally had nothing to do with the experience, so you always can be magnanimous with your empathy and apology.

TIP 221: *Reassure Buyers That Things Have Changed*

You can always start with words: "The situation may have developed when we set up a partnership with Y (or introduced the product line Z). However, that's not an issue now because. . . ."

You should then move beyond the words. You'll need to offer proof—for example, a guarantee of some kind that things have changed; a no-hassle, money-back written guarantee; or no up-front payment until the customer is pleased. You'll want to prove your point with something other than promises.

TIP 222: *Mention Current Customers Who Trust You with Their Business*

Credibility can be earned, won by reputation, or granted by association. After you've lost credibility, your fastest path to regaining it will be to transfer it by association—the link between other satisfied customers who now trust you because you are performing well for them. Focus on that association with clients your prospect admires.

CONCERNS ABOUT RISK

Buyers may fear taking a risk for any number of reasons: What if the competitive product turns out to prove better in the long run? What if the design becomes obsolete? What if the price goes down dramatically immediately after they buy? What if others in the organization don't like what they buy? Can they trust the salesperson to tell them the truth? Can they trust the supplier to stand behind this service or product? The buyers' reason for the risk, of course, will determine in large part how you address it.

TIP 223: *Position Yourself Early On as the "Look Before You Leap" Supplier*

When you make a purchase, various federal and state laws typically allow you from one to five days to change your mind and void a contract. These "right to rescind" clauses in contracts protect buyers from shady transactions and unscrupulous dealers. Buyers use them to void contracts when they discover "surprises" after the sale, such as: "Your free trip to our location doesn't include airfare." "What you thought you *owned* for this fee is really just *licensed.*" "The $1,000 extra coupons you received with your purchase can only be redeemed between 2 AM and 3 AM in Des Moines."

Every industry has its shady suppliers. Additionally, first-time buyers fear going through new processes and facing issues they have not carefully thought through—situations that may create hardships for them after the sale.

All this can work to your advantage.

Early on, position yourself as the low-risk, no-risk supplier by educating customers about shady practices or "must consider" situations *before* they buy. Conduct seminars, hold Webcasts, or write white papers and offer them free to your prospects to educate them about such practices or difficult situations and decisions.

For example, Realtors might prepare a seminar on "Seven Things Homeowners Need to Beware of before Signing the Mortgage Papers"; an insurance salesperson might write a white paper offering "Six Ways Insurance Companies Rip You Off by Selling You Double Coverage"; or a financial planner might present a Webcast titled "What Your Financial Planner Should Tell You—But May Hope You Won't Ask."

Guess who prospects will seek out to handle their next purchase so they're protected and don't have to face such risks?

Of course, if you're in the middle of the sales cycle with a buyer concerned about risk in a particular purchase, then mentioning such past activities and documents will increase your credibility in general. You'll also need to use some of the following tips as well.

TIP 224: *Offer Evidence and Proof*

Webster's dictionary defines evidence as "grounds or information that tends to lead to proof." Proof is defined as "evidence sufficient to establish something as true or a demonstration of truth." In other words, the degree, soundness, or objectivity of evidence leads to its acceptance as proof.

As a salesperson, you can hope your buyers will use the "reasonable test" guideline that judges in our court system explain to jurors: Would a reasonable person consider this information evidence or solid proof of a claim?

The following are all sources of proof—objective, observable, and verifiable:

- Demonstrations of product
- Data from successful projects completed with other clients, with specific references and documentation of results, standards, and testing
- Samples of work
- General independent studies done in the industry, along with information about testing, sampling, or survey questionnaires

The following are considered evidence—sources of information that tend to point toward conclusions, but not hard facts that all would agree on as proof:

- Client lists
- Brand reputation
- Published articles by industry experts
- Testimonial letters

Different buyers will attach varying degrees of importance to these pieces of evidence—some weighing them heavily, while others discounting them altogether. You, of course, hope to have reasonable buyers—like the kind of jurors who sequester themselves in a jury room and come out a few hours later with a sound verdict instead of emerging as a "hung jury."

TIP 225: *Offer a Guarantee—Clever or Straightforward*

If your organization grants you the flexibility to broaden the scope of a guarantee, consider doing so. Often, you're dealing with the perception of risk. In these situations, clever guarantees work just as well.

For example, I used to live in the Panhandle of Texas near a steakhouse on the freeway that advertised an expensive 72-ounce steak dinner with this guarantee: "If you can eat the whole thing, it's free." The risk: "Is this restaurant any good?" The guarantee: "If I don't really like it, I don't have to pay for it." In this case, the guarantee is perception. The steak may not be a gourmet meal and the best you've ever had, but all you have to do is try it out. Even if you don't enjoy it, you don't have to pay for it. At least you won't go away hungry.

A local pharmacist times himself on filling prescriptions: The risk: "If I switch to this pharmacy, will it be too slow?" The guarantee: "If you wait longer than four minutes, you don't owe your co-pay."

Sears became famous for its straightforward "satisfaction guaranteed or your money back" pledge.

Consider how you can remove the risk. If you can't remove the actual risk, can you be clever enough to change the *perception* of risk?

TIP 226: *If You're Not Selling on Commission, Say So*

Buyers often fear that salespeople will tell them anything to make a sale, so customers fear they're "on their own" to ferret out the real truth of any situation. As a teenager, I had an after-school sales job at Sears, where I discovered the magic of this admission. I recall one particular mother who brought her preteen into the store at the beginning of every season to buy her wardrobe. The department manager, who was on commission, tried to talk her into every outfit her daughter tried on. But the chubby little girl had a difficult time finding something flattering. So the first time the mother asked me to give my opinion about the pantsuit the little girl was trying on, I advised her it was unbecoming and suggested something less expensive. In fact, I nixed several choices she was about to buy and directed her to fewer but more becoming styles. I wasn't on commission—I wanted to make a customer happy. On subsequent visits, the mother always asked for me, the sixteen-year-old salesperson, rather than the department manager because she and her daughter trusted my objective opinion.

Buyers look with skepticism at even hard data showing a clear need and cost justification for the purchase, thinking they cannot trust your interpretation. Stating that you make the same salary with or without the sale lends credibility to your analysis and consulting role to the buyer.

TIP 227: *Offer a Specific Timetable to Create Urgency*

Sometimes you have to smoke out risk as the reason for hesitancy because many buyers don't like to admit they're risk-averse. Ask: "How will your situation be different six months down the road?" "After the July meeting with your directors, will you have any new information that you don't have now? If so, I'll plan to call you back that next week to discuss their input on this decision." "Are we still trying to meet your original target date for August installation?"

Such questions lead the buyer to see that the stall is just that—a stall for fear of taking a risk rather than being the "wrong time."

TIP 228: *Offer to Have Another Colleague Handle the Sale for You*

Occasionally, buyers fear making a risky decision when they don't trust you or have confidence in your expertise on the product or service or in your ability to assess their needs. This is particularly true when you're selling a technical product or service to a nontechnical buyer. If they don't trust their own expertise, and they also don't trust yours, the sale is doomed to stall.

Save the sale by stepping out of the picture personally: "Would you be more comfortable in dealing with a colleague on this situation?" If you think trust is low but your buyer may hesitate to call you, suggest a handoff more firmly: "If you don't mind, I'm going to bring Todd Hamilton in on this situation. He's far more experienced than I am on client setups such as yours. I'd like to get his opinion about the efficiencies he expects with this kind of equipment running three shifts."

CONCERNS ABOUT PRODUCT OR SERVICE WEAKNESS

TIP 229: *Acknowledge the Weakness and Counterbalance It with a Benefit*

Don't panic that your buyers will walk away once they realize your product or service has a weakness. Nothing is perfect in a complex sale. Even if the product or service is the best on the market, inevitably execution will be flawed somewhere along the line.

Buyers think rationally for the most part. People marry imperfect spouses. Managers hire imperfect job applicants. Bosses promote imperfect employees. Pet owners love imperfect pets. Families live in imperfect houses. Travelers take less-than-perfect vacations. In all these cases, people see weaknesses and take action anyway because the advantages outnumber the disadvantages.

Your product or service weakness cannot always be repositioned as a strength. You *can*, however, always even the score by adding pluses beside each minus. Your buyers simply need to see both sides of the equation.

TIP 230: *Probe to Determine the Degree of Dismay about Product Limitations*

Some buyers are born to bellyache. They always see the glass half empty, but that doesn't keep them from drinking the water. You need to understand what you're dealing with to determine how much attention to pay to their expressed concern. Probe with "How important is this issue to you?" and go from there. You don't want to hire a surgeon and rent an operating room if you can prescribe two aspirin and ask them to call again in the morning.

TIP 231: *Reposition Your Weakness as a Strength*

You're not trying to "talk buyers out of" what they think, want, or need. Your goal is to give them two perspectives on the issue in question. For example, consider this chart of concerns:

Buyer Concern with What They See as a Product or Service Weakness	Repositioned as a Strength
"This is made of plastic. I thought it was steel. Steel is more durable."	"Yes, we make them of durable plastic so they're more light-weight. They're much more portable that way."
"Your company isn't local. We really prefer dealing with local consultants so they can be on-site quickly."	"Actually, we've considered putting people in the field nearer to our clients. But we've found that most of our tech support is done on the phone anyway. If we have to be on-site, it's only a four-hour flight from anywhere. The significant advantage of our location is that being in the

"You have only one pricing option to include everything—the equipment, customization, installation, delivery, tech support, warranty, and supplies. I don't know that I need all those bells and whistles. I'd rather have just the equipment at a lower price."

Austin area, we can hire the best software expertise in the industry."

"The reason we began pricing it this way was as a convenience to our buyers. We discovered very few technicians had the expertise to customize and install the equipment properly, so they'd try to do both installation and repairs, and it was costing our customers much more in the long run to find their own sources. We decided to add this service arm to ensure that the equipment operates with maximum efficiency—and so you don't have the hassle of finding qualified technicians."

TIP 232: *Position Yourself in the Role of Advisor*

If you agree with the buyers that your product or service is not a good match for their needs, position yourself in the role of consultant and advise them to look elsewhere to meet the need. It is best to lose the sale and keep the potential customer. Be of assistance when you can in referring them to other suppliers. Nothing will build their trust in you as quickly as investing time when you have no immediate vested interest. Yet you have everything to gain by winning their trust for the future.

TIP 233: *Position Yourself as Second Contender for the Future*

Wish buyers well in finding exactly what they want, but suggest that if they don't find a better match with another supplier that they come back to you. Always leave the door open; never make buyers have to lose face to give you a second chance to sell them something.

CONCERNS ABOUT LOYALTY TO ANOTHER SUPPLIER

TIP 234: *Ask What They Like about the Other Supplier and Reposition*

In answering that question, buyers will provide you with their decision criteria. Your next step will be to position your product, service, and organization to those new criteria. Just be careful not to take the "me too" approach in your wording, because at best, you'll score a tie.

If you can't immediately think of ways to reposition yourself on the first approach, then gather information for a second approach: Ask: "When does the contract renew?" "Is there anything at all the buyer would like to change about the supplier's performance or results?" "Is there any related part of the business that the current supplier is not handling or not handling as well as the buyer would like?" "Could you complement what the supplier is doing by adding X, Y, or Z to the service or product line?"

TIP 235: *Question the Criteria or Selection Process*

You should never question the buyer's sound past judgment in selecting the incumbent. It is okay, however, to gently raise issues about "key criteria important to most organizations" in selecting suppliers of X and then mention those. You can "wonder" aloud if X and Y has had input to the decision and if they've examined data from Z to verify the results they're achieving. Finally, you can outline the selection process that many other clients go through in deciding which supplier offers the best results for situations such as theirs. The idea with such questions and discussions will be to lead the buyer subtly to reconsider their past decision or at least tempt them to take another look at current options.

TIP 236: *Create a "Give Us a Try" Appeal*

Avis made the "We're number two; we try harder" theme fashionable. Even the biggest and best in today's economy don't seem to mind this "underdog" plea—it appeals to our sense of fairness.

TIP 237: *Offer to Handle the Dirty Work—Breaking the News*

Some buyers hate giving suppliers the boot so much that they put up with inferior products and service simply because they can't bear to break the bad news.

For others, the issue is not a soft heart, but a weak stomach. They hate the paperwork hassle of transferring their business to a new supplier—preparing new requests for proposals, reviewing the bids, negotiating the contracts, setting up the purchase orders, letting the field staff know, and setting up the online ordering and documentation.

You can take the monkey off their back. Figure out a way to make the transfer of the business easy. Financial institutions have become masters at this: "Just sign on the dotted line, and we'll handle getting your IRAs rolled over to our institution."

CONCERNS ABOUT BEING TOO BUSY

More and more, buyers wear multiple hats and feel they can't squeeze another decision into their day. When you run into a buyer who seems genuinely ready to buy but overwhelmed with the process, consider the tips that follow.

TIP 238: *Emphasize That the Buying Decision Will Alleviate Some of the Workload*

If true, point out that you can ease the buyer's burden with faster service, more efficient delivery, streamlined implementation, less paperwork, better online processing or documentation, one-stop shopping, or a turnkey project. Explain that with one decision, the buyer can, in effect, "outsource" the work to you.

TIP 239: *Suggest the Buyer Delegate the Purchase Decision and Implementation*

Yes, of course, you want to sell to the highest level possible. But if that key person continues to stall, you've gained nothing by being inside the pearly gates. Ask for their blessing and introduction to the level below with a "charge" to move ahead. Then lead the subordinate to "carry out the wishes" of the boss to solve problem X or set a course of action to accomplish Y for the future. Subtly help the subordinate keep in mind the high visibility of such a decision and mission.

TIP 240: *Ask about a Better Schedule*

If neither of the previous tips works, ask your too-busy buyers when their schedules look less busy. This will accomplish one of two things:

They'll give you a future time when things look quieter and you can approach them again at that time, or they'll consider their workload and realize that their current schedule and workload is "normal" and likely to continue indefinitely, in which case they may decide to take a break and *make* the time to buy and implement your solution.

CONCERNS THAT ARE HIDDEN OR UNSTATED

Buyers may have a concern and fear to share it with you. Or they may not fully understand their concern themselves and thus may not be able to articulate it. Still other buyers may not want to state their concern to you for fear you'll invalidate it, ridicule it, or argue with it. Whatever the reason, you can't address the issue if you don't know what it is.

TIP 241: *Make Sure You're Responding to the Real Concern—Not Just the Stated One*

The purpose of a trial close is to check your understanding of previous discussions to determine if your buyer is ready to move ahead to the next stage of the buying process. You're asking for an opinion on what's transpired up to this point. As in any social or business discussion, sometimes you get the buyer's real opinion. Sometimes not.

Examples of trial closes: "What's your time frame on having this equipment installed?" "Do you think you'd lease or buy?" "Are you thinking you'd have us train your equipment operators in-house or send your technicians to our public programs?" "Which model looks more like what you need for your regional office?" "Is this close to what you had in mind?"

If the opinion of your product or service is favorable, you're ready to move on. If the opinion is unfavorable, you need to provide more information or answer more questions. In any case, you need to get at the true opinion so you know what to discuss next.

TIP 242: *Clarify the Vague "I Want to Think It Over"*

Ask: "Do you know what you'll be mulling over as you consider this in the next few days?" "Can you elaborate on what you mean by that?"

TIP 243: *Clarify the Vague "I Want to Look Around"*

Ask: "What exactly do you plan to compare, analyze, or check into further?" "How do mean exactly?"

TIP 244: *Clarify by Reading Their Mind*

Probe with comments such as: "The X issue still seems like it's a concern to you. Is it?" The buyer is either going to confirm that the issue is still a concern and you can discuss it further—or let it go. Either way, you'll know what matter you need to address in more detail in further discussions. The buyer also might put aside the matter altogether, letting you know that the X issue has been resolved in their mind. Now you're one step closer to understanding the situation.

GENERAL GUIDELINES: CLOSING

TIP 245: *Never Bring Up New Information During the Closing Stage*

Bringing up new information related to your product or service at this point will often confuse buyers and send them back to square one in evaluating their options, gaining consensus among multiple buyers, and making a decision. If new information does surface in your buyer's situation, this may necessitate reanalyzing your offering, so that you can provide the best solution.

On the bright side, while not closing the current sale, you may open the door to even bigger opportunities.

TIP 246: *Write a Contract "Subject to Final Approval"*

Some complex sales involving multiple buyers can seem to take forever to close. The same can be true of those sales involving buyers who won't admit they don't have final authority to approve a sale, and yet won't give you access to the real decision maker.

If your contact is on board with your recommendations, suggest that you go ahead and write a contract "subject to final approval." That allows you to put all the provisions in writing and work out all the remaining details while still giving a "safety net" (no final approval yet) to the risk-adverse buyer. Then all that remains is a signature, which requires less action (and ability) on the recommender's part than going in and making a presentation on your behalf.

This principle has worked astoundingly well for book and record clubs for decades—they keep sending you products unless you cancel. Your contract starts the buying process unless the approver refuses to sign.

TIP 247: *Recognize Positive Buying Signals*

Have you ever felt hungry but waited so long to eat that the hunger finally passed? When you're dieting, that's a great realization. When selling, not so. You don't want to arouse your buyer's interest, and then delay the process so long that they lose their inclination to buy before you get around to closing the sale.

To maintain momentum, you have to stay alert to the buyer's mindset. The following signals should get your attention:

- Positive statements about your product or service
- Asking about details of use, price, payment, delivery, or implementation
- Asking about references from other users
- Asking about buying incentives or discounts
- Physically handling the product or testing or demonstrating it
- More relaxed body language and facial expression
- Asking about warranties, return policies, maintenance
- Continually looking at another person (friend, family member, employee) for support in the decision
- Taking copious notes on what you're saying
- Asking lots of questions (buyers ask about what interests them)
- Sudden change of attitude—friendlier, more open
- Moving closer to you physically
- Asking you to repeat information
- Playing with their hair or gadgets (nervous before making final decision)
- Using "ownership" phrases

- Touching chin, covering their mouth, tugging at ear—signals they're thinking, wanting to interrupt you to ask a question/show concern/decide

Taken separately, these signals may mean little, but several together give you a positive picture.

TIP 248: *Be Alert to Signs of Trouble in a Trial Close*

You know the sale has gone awry when you ask for a final commitment and you encounter one of these reactions:

- The prospect begins to ask for more information—particularly about issues that you think you've already explained very well.
- The buyer's mood changes. He or she refuses to talk about the matter any longer or limit answers to brief yes's and no's and their body language changes (tense face; nervous gestures and movements; gestures of dismissal—folded arms, leaning away, backing up, putting barriers between you such as doorways, desks, briefcases, or stacks of papers).

These are flashing red signs that probably should have caught your attention miles down the road. Something has happened. Don't try to blare your horn and move through the intersection. Stop. Do not pass go.

Questions are in order to get the conversation back on track. If the buyer is asking for more information, answer the questions briefly and then say: "You and I have discussed these issues several times before and I thought we had nailed down all the concerns you had. It seems like we're moving backward now, and you're beginning to doubt some of the conclusions your technical experts drew in previous meetings. Help me understand what's happened since our last meeting?"

In the case of no talking and a mood change: "I sense a complete change in our interactions. I don't feel that you're as interested as you were. Have I done something wrong here or left something undone? Please feel free to level with me. That's how I learn—from my mistakes."

Then listen.

TIP 249: *Motivate Rather Than Manipulate*

Your buyer may have moved along with you so seamlessly in the process that both of you just assume that you will do business together and automatically move to finalize the paperwork and implement the sale. If that happens, great.

If not, you may elect to use various closing techniques to lead the buyer to take the next steps rather than to delay. Leading means providing motivation and direction—but not manipulation.

TIP 250: *Assume the Close*

Start asking about the details, assuming the buyer is planning to move ahead.

TIP 251: *Provide Alternatives to Close*

Some buyers pause at every fork in the road and wait for direction. Assume the buyer has moved along with you through the discussion and will be willing to take the step, given two choices: "Do you think Model X or Model Y would suit your needs better?" "Are you thinking your technicians would prefer to handle the installation themselves, or would that be something you'd like our people to handle?" "Would a meeting next week or the end of the month be better for your team to discuss the details of our proposal and the implementation plan?"

TIP 252: *Take Buyers for a "Test Drive" to Close*

This "test drive" close has also been called the puppy dog close or the pilot close. The idea is to let your buyers try out or sample your product or service before they buy. Car dealerships let you take the car for a test drive on the highway. Copier dealers set up their machines for your use for a couple of months, hoping you'll grow dependent on them. Wireless phone companies and cable companies give you a month's free service to let you experience their service and equipment. Lawyers provide free consultations.

Investigate ways you can let your buyers "experience" your solution before they have to commit permanently.

TIP 253: *Bridge from the Buyer's Question to Close*

The buyer's question: "How long does it take to get it delivered and installed? I'd need it by July." Your bridge: "If you'd like me to write the order today, I could get it to the manufacturer by the end of the week. Delivery would take three weeks. Installation another two weeks. That means we could definitely have it in place by July. Shall I move ahead with the order so we don't miss your target date?"

TIP 254: *Use the Ben Franklin Checklist to Close*

Ben Franklin was known for making decisions by getting out a piece of paper and listing all the pros and cons in checklist form. You may want to do the same with your buyers: The choices may be "buy now" versus "buy later" or "buy stripped-down version" versus "buy super-duper model" or "hire us for the project" versus "do the project with internal staff." Then help your buyer think through the process to arrive at the decision to move ahead with the purchase.

TIP 255: *Summarize and Be Silent to Close*

Sum up your offering, recap the benefits and the value—those real advantages meaningful to your buyer—and then be quiet. Silence calls for response. Buyers will often take the next step themselves, suggesting that you finalize the sale or asking you what the next step should be. It's your job to tell them.

TIP 256: *Ask for a Reaction to Close*

Your approach may be straightforward and somewhat formal: "I hope I've been clear in my overview. I want your business. May I write up the order?" "It seems as though you have no more questions. Can we consider this agreed?" "Are you ready to sign the contract and notify the other branches that the purchase order will be in effect by the end of the month?"

You can be casual: "So what do you think?" "How does all this sound to you?" "Does this make sense in your location?" "Just what the doctor ordered in your predicament, right?" "On a scale of one to ten, where would you say you and your team are in making this decision—ready to move ahead with the contract?" "So are you ready to get started with the project? We could begin as early as next week." "If you're ready to roll, I'll notify the appropriate people in my office and we'll get the ball on down the court." "Ready to move ahead?" "Would you like for me to start the process for you?" "I recommend that we start the process Friday. How does that sound?" "Tell me where you'd like to start." "I need your signature on this authorization to get the process started." "Okay, what's our next step here in your office to get the rest of the team ready to implement?" "Where would you like to go from here?" "So how do we proceed with approaching the branch offices to get them aboard?" "What would you recommend as a first step in approaching your headquarters to let them know you want this formalized as soon as possible?" "What do we need to do first to get this underway formally here?" "Anything standing in our way here?"

GUIDELINES: RESPONDING WHEN LOSING A SALE

TIP 257: *Read Early Signs of Problems*

Sometimes it's all too easy to bury our head in the sand and not see waves rolling in and creating turmoil in a sales relationship. Usually, the waves don't just hit the shore suddenly without warning. Some of the more typical waves you may experience include having the buyer resurface issues you thought had already been addressed or postpone the buying decision again and again. They may refuse to meet with you with no plausible reason, withhold information that typically is shared with suppliers, or fail to respond to your phone calls or e-mails.

Sometimes, more violent waves develop: seeing the competitors' literature lying around; having your projects put out for competitive bids; learning the decision-making authority and hierarchy have been altered.

If you're in the water when bad weather threatens, adjust your sails and strategy accordingly.

TIP 258: *Respond to Resurfacing of the Same Issues Raised and Addressed*

Be direct. Your tone will make the difference in whether this works or sounds impatient, so take care with inflection as well as phrasing when you discuss this issue. Example: "Heather, I'm puzzled about why the issue of customizing has resurfaced again from your HR staff. After we talked about that last month in the meeting with Sanford and Jana, I thought we had answered everyone's concerns and had come to consensus that customization wasn't going to be necessary on this project. Can you help me understand *what has changed* since that last discussion?" Then listen carefully.

TIP 259: *Respond to Postponements without Reasons*

Buyers will be fuzzy about how often they've postponed a meeting, so you'll need to be specific to get a straight answer as to why. Take care, however, that you don't adopt a "you did it to me" tone. Example: "I understood from the outset that your target date for a decision was July. Then we had to postpone our May 2 meeting. Then May 16. And June 16 turned out not to be a good date either. Can you let me know what has been happening behind the scenes that has affected this decision?"

Your buyers may or may not be forthcoming with specifics. If they're not, try a further probe: "How do things stand now? What's your new time line?" If they're still vague, follow up with, "Can you tell me where I've gotten off track? Should we be doing something differently? Do we need to discuss some new concerns?"

TIP 260: *Respond to Unwillingness to Meet*

Unwillingness to meet can mean good news (efficiency—the buyer doesn't want to waste your time or theirs in unnecessary meetings until there's a problem with implementation plans that needs to be solved) or bad news. Ask outright: "I've suggested that we meet several different times and you haven't thought that necessary. I don't know if I should consider that good news or bad news. Good news that everything's on track as we've discussed—so there's no need to spend your valuable time meeting, or bad news that things are off track and undecided again. Which would you say it is? Good news or bad news that we don't need to meet?"

Such a question begs for elaboration. This also will give you a fighting chance to address hidden issues.

TIP 261: *Respond to Withholding Information*

Be direct by stating what you think is happening, explain how that affects your ability to offer the best solutions, and ask for verification of the situation. Example: "It seems that earlier in our discussions, you were able to provide much more detail about your situation, your criteria for making this decision, and your expectations about X. Recently, however, I've needed information on Y to enable me to gather the best ideas from our engineering team to design the best approach to include in our proposal. I've felt the information I've been receiving—specifically about X—has been limited. Am I mistaken?"

In a formal bidding process, of course, you always can submit such information requests in writing and force the liaison in charge of the project to respond to all bidders with the answers. The danger, however, is in tipping your hand to your competitors.

TIP 262: *Respond to Unreturned Calls and Unanswered E-mails*

Often, assuming the worst and responding graciously shames the buyer out of rudeness and generates a response. Write a "sorry we weren't selected, but we wish you well with the project" letter. Nine times out of ten, if buyers have not yet made a final decision and have delayed in letting you know just because they have "no news," such a letter generates an immediate phone call. Typically, they apologize that they've had to postpone the decision for one reason or another, saying they've hated to contact you because they knew you'd be disappointed that no decision has been reached. Then they give you an update. That puts you in the position of either helping them to reach a decision or disqualifying them and moving on to another opportunity.

TIP 263: *Respond to Discovering Competitive Literature in Your Buyer's Work Area*

A humorous and light approach works well. Examples: "Looks as though you're trying to keep me awake nights." "Uh oh. I see Brand X on the shelf. I'd better do a good job today, hadn't I?" "I see traces of competitive literature lying around. I sure hope you're not big into those reality TV game shows—where they let competitors fight to the death?"

Then transition to a serious discussion: "Seriously, I'd like to have the opportunity to address all your concerns. Give me our report card. How are we doing so far in meeting your needs?" Notice the *we* phrasing. Buyers may have a difficult time telling you personally how *you're* handling their account, but if you give them permission to tell you how *your organization* stacks up against the opposition, they may feel more comfortable in sharing hidden concerns and issues you can address. And that's your goal.

TIP 264: *Respond to a Change in Structure or Decision Makers*

Before you decide whether to be happy or sad about the change, ask your contact their assessment of the new situation: "How do you feel about the change?" If they seem distressed about it (and were in your corner earlier), then you have new trouble brewing.

Ask for coaching about the next steps. If they are noncommittal regarding the change, it may be either a face-saving answer on their part or a change they've instigated to avoid responsibility and risk. In that case, pursue with this line of probes: "Is this purchase a higher or lower priority for your organization currently?" "What new risks do you think [new decision maker] will see in the situation?" "Which of the key payoffs will be of the most interest to him or her?" "The least?" "Why do you think the decision is now being handled by the X department/person/division?"

Your goal with such questioning is to encourage the contact-turned-advisor to spill guarded information under the guise of sharing perceptions about *someone else's* thoughts and priorities—which is always safer than sharing their own. Of course, you will understand that people tend to see things through their own colored lenses. But having any negative information sooner rather than later gives you time to correct those perceptions.

TIP 265: *Thank the Buyer for Considering Your Offer*

Buyers have choices on most products and services, and they do not have to spend their time with you. Situations change often: buyers find more money; decision makers change and influencers move to new organizations; risk-adverse people gain courage; corporations merge; and sellers lose their jobs and need new ones.

Word of rudeness and sour grapes travels fast in most industries.

TIP 266: *Follow Up to Discover Why You Lost the Sale*

Following up your losses may be even more important than learning from your wins. Winning may be redundant. Losing shouldn't be.

When you ask your buyer why you lost the sale, take care to phrase your question in a nonconfrontational way: "I'm sure you've given this decision careful thought. We like to learn from our mistakes. Is there something we could and should have done different that would have changed the outcome or altered the decision?" Listen and learn.

TIP 267: *Leave the Door Open*

Avoid being pushy or overeager. Ask for permission to stay in touch periodically with updates on your product or service or to share industry news. Few will turn you down. Then do so. You can share a common interest, information from a peer, or congratulate them on happenings in their own organization.

You want to be first in line if the competition falters or the situation changes in other ways.

TIP 268: *Ask for a Referral While They Feel Obligated*

Prospects sometimes feel bad when the conditions—no authority or budget—won't let them buy. In fact, on occasion, they even regret that a competitor had a better product match because they genuinely like you as a person. When that's the case, don't pass up the opportunity to ask for a referral to their colleagues. Prospects in such situations may work doubly hard to come up with names for you. They often give glowing referrals about your attention to detail during the sales cycle and even about your product, telling the colleague that their needs were different or budget was limited, and if they'd had a bigger budget they would have bought the superior product—yours.

TIP 269: *Move On to Other Opportunities*

Understand that rejection is rarely personal. Buyers don't respond for any number of reasons: No money. No need. No urgency. No desire. No understanding of value. No push to change from the status quo. So accept no graciously. Rejection lasts only as long as you let it. As with games and sports, move on and celebrate your next success.

5

NEGOTIATING FOR LONG-TERM LOYALTY

Utter the word *negotiate* and some sales professionals conjure up images as diverse as street vendors in Hong Kong, oil sheiks in the Middle East, and horse trading in Kansas. Other sales professionals insist they're given no flexibility at all in working out prices and contract provisions with buyers. Yet weekly they make deals that look very different from buyer to buyer.

In today's marketplace where every buyer is looking for "a deal," how do you respond without losing the sale while protecting your profit margin? Tips in this chapter will help you to hold your own.

TIP 270: *Reset Buyer Expectations Early in the Sales Process*

Many buyers enter a sales discussion with some idea of what they expect to pay for a product or service—either from a previous price they've paid, from an ad they've seen, from a colleague talking in the hallway, or from their "wish" list or budget (no matter whether that wish list is based on reality or ignorance). It will be to your advantage to lead them to reality as soon as you have established the value of your offering or solution— preferably before you begin any negotiation.

TIP 271: *Reset Expectations with Questions Instead of Statements*

Statements may seem shocking and lead to a confrontational reaction. Questions, on the other hand, typically come across as a matter-of-fact exchange of information. If you prefer, support your point using an off-the-cuff offer of an article, recent research or statistics about trends, prices, values, and so forth. Example: "Have you seen the recent article in *FRG Journal* about the rising costs associated with this new process for filtering?" Such a question puts the customer on notice early on in the discussion about current prices and increases throughout the industry.

TIP 272: *"Review" Your Price Quote with Your Sponsor Before You "Finalize" It*

In a complex sale containing several provisions and add-ons and where you have some flexibility in pricing, set up a meeting to discuss other issues during which you give the sponsor opportunity to bring up pricing as a sidebar. Explain that you want to "run through the various options" that you've tentatively put together to make sure everything is complete before you do a formal draft or agreement.

With your buyer, run through the list of the various options you plan to include in the package. Beside each option, have the price listed. If the buyer questions the price on any item, you can pause to explain or discuss it. If no questions surface, you can assume that the numbers in your final pricing arrangement will be no surprise.

TIP 273: *Never Offer a Discount as an Incentive to Buy*

A discount may increase a customer's desire to buy or entice a customer to buy something more frequently or to buy sooner. Discounts, however, cannot create a need or interest in the first place. In fact, discounts often have the opposite effect.

Consider your reaction when you're shopping at the open-air markets found around the world. You see a jacket priced at $250. You shrug your shoulders and say, "I don't know if I really need a jacket."

The merchant replies, "I'll give you $50 off."

Your reaction is to wonder, What's wrong with the jacket? "No, I don't think I need the jacket."

The merchant then says, "I'll make you a good deal: Half off. $125."

"No, thank you," you reply and start to walk away.

The merchant calls after you, "Genuine leather. Only $100."

If your buyer has no real desire to buy, dropping the price will not help.

TIP 274: *Reverse the Buyer's Logic on Risk*

When buyers don't understand the value of the various options you offer, it often helps to lead them gently to reason in the opposite direction. For example, let's say a buyer asks you to offer a lower price because their organization has had such a bad year. You might respond by asking if they would be willing to sign a contract to pay a premium next year if the company has a more profitable year.

Another example: Let's say you're selling computer consulting services and you quote a price and agree to a completion date for the project. The client insists that having the project completed on time is essential to their success and wants to build in a penalty clause to ensure that you meet the project deadline. The penalty clause says your firm forfeits a 5 percent penalty fee for every week you miss the deadline. You, on the other hand, hesitate to add the clause because you know many things outside your control can affect the deadline. In this case, you might reverse the buyer's logic: Would they be willing to add a clause to pay your firm a 5 percent per week bonus for completing the project early?

Simply adjust the control or circumstances of the situation so that the buyer understands the risk you're assuming and the value you're offering.

TIP 275: *Never Assume That Because Buyers Ask for a Discount They Expect One*

Some organizations require that their purchasing agents request a discount as a matter of course. They simply need assurance that they're being quoted your best price.

TIP 276: *Differentiate between Price Justification and Price Negotiation*

Understand the difference between a buyer's price justification questions and comments and the price negotiation stages of a sale. Price justification questions and comments are those asking you to show the value of your offering. Buyers ask them when they're not sure they want or need your product or service.

Price negotiation comments and questions, on the other hand, indicate the buyer has committed to buy and wants what you offer. The buyer asks questions or makes comments to see what concessions you might be willing to make.

Offering concessions too early—as an incentive to buy—is costly and useless.

TIP 277: *State Your Price and Be Silent*

Silence is a powerful tool in negotiating. Buyers need time to align the information with their expectations and justify the price against the expected outcomes. Just wait.

At times, of course, you may come to a deadlock. You've stated your price and remained silent, and your buyer has done the same. The buyer refuses to engage in further dialogue. They won't make a decision and agree on your price, and neither will they make a counteroffer. Typically, in a deadlock, the first person to break the silence usually concedes.

Talking after you state the price sets up several dangers: You may sound defensive and set up a confrontational tone; you may unintentionally plant the idea that you're expecting to have to discount the price; or, you may create the impression that you routinely have to "talk your buyer into" the price. None of these is a good reason for talking about your price.

In a situation when your buyer seems to be stonewalling on a decision about your stated price but refusing to make a counteroffer, you have two next options. First, you can ask for a specific when your buyer is vague with a comment such as "That won't work" or "That seems too high." Second, you can withdraw your quote or proposal. You can put a time limit on it or move on to other clients and divert your attention to let a buyer know you don't intend to modify the offer.

TIP 278: *Help Buyers Justify the Price in Their Own Minds*

Help buyers see how your package and situation differs from those in the past and from what may come up in the future.

TIP 279: *Help Your Buyers Justify the Price to Other Colleagues*

If you've been persuasive and led your buyers to agree to your asking price for your initial package, then buyers have to do so without embarrassment. They have to be able to go back to their colleagues and explain why they agreed to buy from you—at full price or at a price higher than your competitors—and feel good about it. Help them explain the situation and the value.

TIP 280: *Negotiate When That's Your Only Alternative*

Salespeople typically arrive at the conclusion to negotiate far too early. You should negotiate when your only alternative is to lose the business, and when you will gain something in return. How do you know definitively when you're about to lose the business? Sometimes your buyers will tell you directly, and only your relationship and your gut will tell you when to believe them. Sometimes you have to read their actions or inactions to know.

In either case, that's only half the equation. Before you think negotiation or trade, consider what you have to gain. Can you hope to trade for a large enough profit margin to make it worth your trouble? What do you stand to gain by having this prestigious buyer on your client list? Are they a good beta site for a new service?

Consider both conditions before you start the negotiation process.

TIP 281: *Understand That Negotiating Price Lessens Your Credibility*

Concessions cost your credibility. When you offer discounts easily and quickly, clients often feel just the opposite from what you expect.

They feel distrustful—that your first offer was deceptive; that your product is worth less than you first asked; that you price things on subjective feelings and might not be giving them the best deal possible.

Their reasoning goes like this: If you give away reductions so easily, does that mean they were about to be taken by paying full price?

Giving price concessions early can decrease your profit so much so that some situations become a loss instead of a win. Collaborative selling means that both you and the buyer must win, and that means you and your organization must make a reasonable profit to be able to deliver a quality product or service.

TIP 282: *Think "Trade," Not "Discount"*

Instead of conceding on price, think trade. Ask for something of value to you in return for the price concession. First, you may get what you want—a bigger order, a longer contract, add-on business lines. Second, suggesting a trade—whether you end up with the trade or not—elevates the importance of what you give to the buyer in return. Finally, asking for trades reduces the chance the buyer will ask you for other discounts and concessions.

TIP 283: *Distinguish between Your Primary Goals and Secondary Goals before Any Negotiations*

Jot down your primary goals, which are exactly what you *must* walk away with—your nonnegotiable items and issues. For example, a 9 percent profit margin; payment within ten days; the project scheduled and completed before first quarter ends. Next, identify your secondary goals—what you'd *like* to have but might be willing to trade. For example, you might like to have payment within ten days, but you could offer a trade—say, a 30-day payment schedule in return for a larger order from your customer.

Finally, develop your trade list. Consider what you have of value that you could trade to get what you want and then determine what you want to ask from the buyer as a trade if they ask for a concession on price, delivery, or payment schedule.

TIP 284: *Identify Your Buyer's Primary Goals and Potential "Trades" List*

To negotiate win-win deals, you have to understand what your buyer values. Consider the trading list of your favorite pro sports team. The team owner might pay twice the price for a good pitcher as he or she pays for a shortstop—it depends on what's needed.

From previous conversations, you should know what your buyer values most. During the negotiation phase, you will ask for trades based on those items. For example: extended delivery time; up-front payment; flexibility in scheduling; referrals or endorsements; sponsorships at industry events or marketing opportunities; larger volume purchases; multi-year contracts; buyer pick-up instead of delivery; use of the buyer's facility or team for the production/project; or coventure development.

TIP 285: *Identify Your Walk-Away Points*

Even though you've already identified your primary goals (your must haves) and secondary goals (what you'd like to have but may be willing to trade), it helps to use another label for these must haves: walk-away points. In negotiations, you sometimes lose track of what's happening—particularly when savvy buyers wait until the last moment to let these showstoppers crop up in the discussions.

For example, let's say your buyer has known the price of your solution all along, and you have negotiated several matters about delivery, implementation, and customization. When you're ready to sign contracts, however, the buyer lowers the quantity on the order, affecting your profit margin dramatically. The buyer has known your price all along, and you have negotiated all the other issues based on the assumption of a certain order size and price. You are now below your walk-away point.

In such situations, it's far easier to have recast in your mind your primary goal as your "walk-away point" to see you through the emotional crisis.

TIP 286: *Identify All the Buyer's Issues Up Front Before You Negotiate*

Ask buyers for everything they want—all their goals—before you start to put together an agreement. Starting too early means that you may give away too much, only to have additional wants and issues surface later that will cause you to have to make further concessions or lower your profit margins even further.

TIP 287: *Ask Questions to Discover What Buyers Value and Understand about Your Offer*

Questions let you exchange needs and strategic information, and they let you control the conversation without seeming overbearing. Questions give both you and the buyer time to think and to suggest ideas and paths to solutions. If you don't know what your buyers value, you won't know how much a "trade" is worth.

TIP 288: *Lead Buyers to Invest Time and Effort*

Don't rush. The more time and effort your buyers have spent with you, the greater the motivation to work things out and come to an agreement. Make finishing the deal easy and starting over a headache.

TIP 289: *Take Notes*

The effort to take notes shows that you care "to get things right." It also serves as a subtle reminder to your buyers about points you've agreed on and prevents later misunderstandings when you can turn back to your notes and reference a phrase or comment the buyers made earlier.

TIP 290: *Separate Understanding from Agreement*

Occasionally, when you're nodding, smiling, questioning, or writing notes, buyers may understand these affirmations as signs of agreement to what they're requesting. So take care during your discussion to differentiate between statements and body language that mean "I hear you," "I'm following you," "I understand what you're saying," versus "I'm agreeing to this." Otherwise, you may end your discussion with very upset buyers, who feel that you have accepted and agreed to various issues or goals they've stated when, in fact, you may have only meant "I hear you and I wish I could, but I can't" as they were speaking.

TIP 291: *Send Up Trial Balloons Before You "Get Serious"*

If you have something that the buyer may consider a little unusual, you can always pose that trade or solution as an off-handed suggestion and get their reaction. Examples: "Well, you know we could always just. . . ." "Frankly, the best way around all these issues would be to. . . ." If the buyer chokes, you'll be glad you didn't pose the solution as a "real" consideration. If the other person picks up the idea and plays with it, you can treat it seriously.

TIP 292: *Reduce Resistance to "Precedent Setting"*

Sometimes buyers fear setting a precedent for other people in their organization or for later dealings with you. You hear comments such as: "But if I don't require you to do X, none of our suppliers will want to do X." To reduce this pressure on your buyers, you'll need to find a way to help them justify in their own mind how the current situation differs from others that may arise later. That difference becomes the crucial difference.

TIP 293: *Set a Mutually Beneficial, Not Adversarial, Tone*

Words carry weight. People don't always choose them well, but they expect others to. A wrongly chosen word can derail a sale very quickly. For example, to some people the word "negotiate" itself implies to give up something, to compromise. It implies a winner and a loser. Instead, talk about "coming to an agreement," "working out a plan," or "arriving at a workable solution."

Use "fair" and "reasonable" with care. What's "fair" will always be determined by each person's own situation, viewpoint, and values. When you utter the words reasonable or fair, what the buyer hears you say is that any other opinion is "unfair" or "unreasonable."

Also, pay attention to the tone. Consider the difference in how these pairs of sentences come across:

"You'll need to come up with $30,000 before we can begin the custom design work."
"Can you allocate the $30,000 for us to begin the custom design work?"

"We can't deliver it until after the 15th."
"Will delivery after the 15th be a problem for you?"

"The logical solution here is for you to order the first 5,000 units by Friday to get the price break from the manufacturer on the introductory order."

"Ordering the first 5,000 units by Friday will allow you to take advantage of the price break on the introductory offer by the manufacturer."

"That's all I can do."

"Will that work for you?"

The first statement in each pair will guide the discussions to where you need to go—but the second versions will leave a much better taste in the buyer's mouth.

TIP 294: *Negotiate as a Team, Not as Individuals*

Whether intentionally or unintentionally, buyers may divide your sales or technical team, talking first to you and then to someone on your support team separately to press for different concessions from each of you. This happens most often when several members of your team interact with the buyers routinely during the sales cycle—and particularly when you're the incumbent and have ongoing projects with the client. Sometimes buyers talk to your sales managers or even to your other clients when they ask for references. Their idea is to gather information about arrangements you *could* make and deals you have done and new offers you *might* be willing to make if they only ask.

So buyers ask, and it's your job to respond appropriately for your own organization.

When difficulties arise, as the salesperson in charge, you'll need to ask questions of both parties involved to determine exactly who asked or offered what, and who agreed or accepted what. If a member of your team conceded something or added something to an offer, you'll have a difficult time "taking it back" at this point.

You can clarify misinformation shared or correct information misunderstood before agreeing to any concessions. You'll also want to clear up any misconception that you've dealt unfairly with a buyer or supplied any wrong or deceptive information. As the salesperson, you have the last word—not your support-team staff. After you've gathered all the information, clarify and restate your offer so that you incorporate any new details or issues raised by secondary conversations.

Finally, try to prevent such a situation with prior planning: have all team members keep complete notes; when things change, keep all members updated; review all team members' notes for accuracy and thoroughness before you make your first offer; and always ask your team members to do all their negotiating through you.

It's generally not a good idea, however, to make a blanket statement that you prefer buyers speak only to you and not to your team members. First, buyers don't like orders. Second, they will become suspicious. And third, such an arrangement will often be impossible to maintain.

A team provides support—they're there to back you up, to answer technical questions, to lend credibility. Both your team and your buyers may feel insulted with such a blanket statement. Instead, try to prevent the divide-and-conquer problem by making your team aware of the consequences of seemingly "minor" comments and off-handed information, and ask for their cooperation in directing those issues back to you.

Divided, you fall. United, you get the best package—with your profit in place.

TIP 295: *Beware the Absent Decision Maker*

Buyers often insist that they have no authority to make a final decision —that a committee, team, or boss must approve the purchase. Even when they may technically have the final "say so," they may abdicate that authority to others to give technical opinions or user input. In any case, the effect is the same: You are "one down" because you can't negotiate and ask for a trade from someone who isn't present. Therefore, everything you offer becomes a starting point for the next round of discussions.

To avoid being put in this one-down circumstance, clarify up front who has the final authority in any given buying situation, and then make sure you're making every effort to speak directly to that person or group. You also can appeal to a buyer's ego—lead the buyer to confirm authority before you get to the point of decision.

Finally, you can offer to close the deal, with a time-limited "out" clause, pending final approval. That is, offer to put everything in writing and suggest the deal be approved conditionally by offering a clause that lets the buyer opt out within a specified time frame for whatever reason that seems to be the hang-up—until the powers-that-be have a chance to approve it. The buyer now has automatically said yes until the boss or committee goes to the extra trouble to say no and "undo" the deal.

To sum up: It's not necessarily that buyers intend to be cagey about their authority; many just don't want to be confrontational by telling you directly what they're thinking. It's the process itself that exerts pressure on you from the very beginning to offer your very lowest price to "win approval" by the unseen authority.

It's up to you to recognize that pressure and respond appropriately.

TIP 296: *Don't Fall Victim to the Good Guy, Bad Guy Routine with Your Sponsor*

This negotiation strategy works in tandem with the absent decision maker. It involves having one person act as your "sponsor" who wants to do business with you, but pleads with you for your best offer to convince others. Occasionally, this sponsor is "assigned" by the organization to be your liaison, contact, and encourager throughout the bidding process. On other occasions, the sponsor is acting on their own accord and genuinely prefers your organization and wants to see you win the business.

The first step in responding to such a strategy is to determine if the Good Guy sponsor has a genuine interest in seeing you win the business. That's where your interpersonal skills come into play. Do they show evidence of emotional connection to the outcome? Do they "go the extra mile" when you ask for help? Are they willing to spend time with you in collecting information and putting together an excellent proposal? What's the depth of their answers to your questions? The answers to these questions definitely shed light on intentions.

If you identify the sponsor as someone who has been "assigned" and not necessarily interested in your organization, stand your ground. Rejustify your offer, but don't necessarily let down your guard and follow their advice about what you "must do" to win favor with the missing Bad Guy.

If, on the other hand, you determine that the Good Guy genuinely prefers your organization, instead of modifying your terms to what they say will be acceptable to the Bad Guy, offer to go with the Good Guy to meet the Bad Guy head on to justify your value and explain your offer. If the Good Guy says that's not possible, do all you can to help them help you by providing credentials, evidence, information, competitive analysis, and the like.

TIP 297: *Never Let Your Buyers Know You Have Final Say-So*

Although you want your clients to know you're credible and successful at what you do, you're at a distinct disadvantage when you claim to be the final decision maker—even when you are. Conferring with others before you can alter pricing or terms or offer additional concessions or options is always a good idea. The "others" involved may mean a boss, a team, a committee, the marketing department, your executive group, your board, your lawyer, your CPA, the owner, your subordinates, your staff, or your spouse. Just somebody other than you. Concessions surface as another case where it gets lonely at the top, and being boss can be next to no fun and near disaster where negotiation is concerned.

This consultation process has several advantages: It gives you time to think. It makes the concession seem more important and valuable. It can preserve the relationship with the buyer, making someone else the "bad guy" if you must say no. It often prevents buyers from arguing with you and pressing you to change your mind if they know it was a group decision. On occasion, some buyers grow impatient waiting for you to get approvals from different levels of management for concessions and buy anyway—without the concessions. Finally, the process conveys to the buyer that you don't routinely give concessions, which, in turn, makes them value the concession even more.

All these situations and perceptions can give you leeway in a negotiation. If you do come back to your buyer with a concession, you'll make them feel special and more inclined to offer a concession in return.

Bragging that you have final say on a sale may be great for the ego— but bad for the bottom line.

TIP 298: *Beware of Red Herrings*

Buyers sometimes pose an obstacle to the sale that's not the real issue but a red-herring issue meant as a decoy. The buyer will then offer to concede on that issue—if you'll agree to do X, which is the real agenda. Be sure to ask questions, probe, and listen for what's not said. Sidestep the minor issue and wait for the big one.

TIP 299: *Don't Run for Cover during a Bomb Scare*

The buyer may drop an unexpected decision, a change, or bad news at the last minute in the hope that you will make concessions quickly to keep a deal on track. When your buyer drops a bomb, don't panic and scramble to modify your offer. Instead, pause and reassess the situation, and then select a more appropriate response.

Ask: "Is that the only obstacle?" Make sure you've isolated the only thing holding you back from closing the sale. Asking this question and listening to the answer often helps you determine if the "bomb" is real or simply a negotiation strategy.

If you determine that it is real, ask: "Who can change things?" Get others involved. Develop alternatives to check out the assumptions being made about the new situation. Look for higher levels of authority that know more about the bomb and can detonate it.

Finally, remember that occasionally the bomb scare is just that: a sudden change of events on the way to a closed deal. Don't automatically assume the issue is price and start scrambling to offer discounts. Instead, focus on removing the obstacle—without altering your proposed terms.

TIP 300: *Keep Your Cool When Buyers Give You a Ticking-Clock Ultimatum*

Deadlines represent reality. But they represent reality for *two* people—the buyer and the seller. If a buyer tries to use a deadline as an ultimatum, you may want to reverse the pressure.

Point out ever so gently the buyer's *own* disadvantages in delaying a decision. Talk up the advantages of an early decision such as cheaper prices from your own suppliers that you can pass on to the buyer; price increases announced for future dates; security of scheduling; faster solutions to their own problems; quicker reduction in their waste and costs; or faster growth in their revenues that your solution will generate.

In short, never be deceptive about deadlines to create pressure for a buyer. Tactfully point out, however, that deadlines affect both buyers and sellers.

TIP 301: *Reverse the Pressure of a Ticking Clock*

Sometimes buyers state a deadline—real or arbitrary—as if it's an ultimatum to create pressure for a quick decision from you on a concession. They may also let other "crucial" decision points pass in silence to create fear and pressure that you have lost the deal, and to signal that they may not intend to buy after all your effort. Their hope is that you will panic and offer a concession to seal the deal.

The attitude of "let's get it done" can wreak havoc. Give yourself time to generate the best agreement. When the buyer asks for a concession, wait. This simple concept may be your saving virtue. State that if you must give an immediate answer, your first response must be no unless you have more time, for example, to "consider the situation," "check with your manager," or "verify some other information" before you can determine if there's a "maybe" response.

TIP 302: *Be Wary of "Cherry Pickers"*

Rather than looking at overall price, sometimes buyers attempt to negotiate item by item. Each individual supplier, however, puts together their package in a different way and may build their profit into a different part of the project or product.

An appropriate response to cherry-picking buyers is to put them on the spot—nicely, of course. They like to ask you to break down your bid item by item so they can question each amount, determine your costs, and then calculate your profit item by item. In the questioning, their hope is to save a few dollars here and there, or, better, to get you to agree to match the low bid on each item.

Instead of assuming that your *total* bid was high, simply call the buyer's hand on this issue with a straightforward question: "Is our *total* price higher than all the other competing suppliers?" You also can ask it in another way: "Are all the competing bids lower than ours in *all* areas? Different firms allocate their costs and profits in different ways."

Force your buyers to make apples-to-apples comparisons. Don't automatically assume their apples-to-oranges inferences mean that you need to lower your bid.

After determining that your buyer is intending to select different suppliers for each aspect of a project, you might want to let the buyer do just that. If your price is "too high" on one item, suggest that the buyer remove that item from the table and consider your organization for the remainder of the project. Chances are great that the buyer will decide that the trouble of cherry picking—dealing with and coordinating multiple suppliers, which often leads to delays, interruptions, and more administrative work—is much more trouble than a slightly higher fee on one single aspect of a bid.

With Cherry Pickers, stand firm on your price and sell the whole load.

TIP 303: *Take Care Not to Set False Expectations in "Last Match" Situations*

When buyers tell you you're the high bidder and offer you an opportunity to "take another look at your numbers," take care that you haven't set up false expectations in their minds. If you come back with the same quote, your response will be framed as a disappointment. Often, you'd do well to determine if your *overall* bid was actually higher than the bid from competitors.

On occasion, you may want an opportunity to match an overall lower bid. In those situations, you might consider a direct but tactful approach: "Are you at liberty to tell me what price I'd have to quote to remain under consideration?" If buyers want to deal with you, they'll sometimes tell you exactly what price you have to match. You also might phrase the question this way: "Are you saying that price is your primary consideration at this point?" If they say no, rejustify your value.

TIP 304: *Be Wary of "Also Ran" Requests for Proposals*

Occasionally, buyers may encourage you through the sales process—only to take your offer to a preferred supplier to get that supplier to lower their price. Yet, it's difficult to be sure you're being used in this way and you never want to miss a legitimate opportunity. Finding out the following information can help you determine if you're being used as a foil:

- Elaborate on your qualifications for the job and then probe about which of those holds the most interest for the buyer.
- Ask who else is under consideration.
- Ask about any incumbent and probe about why the buyer is considering a switch.
- Determine how much time the buyer is willing to invest in providing information to you to help you prepare your offer.

This information will provide insight about the legitimacy of the opportunity.

TIP 305: *Be Wary about Matching the Foil*

Sometimes the previous negotiating strategy has a happier twist—your competitor is the foil and you are the preferred supplier. The buyers may begin negotiations with other suppliers to get their best deal. Next, the buyers ask you to match that low price.

When that's the situation, before scrambling to respond with a match, take time to assess how the value your firm brings to the table stacks up against the competition. Probe for revealing details about the buyers' criteria and how other bidders stack up.

Discover why you've been giving the "matching privilege" last. Probe about who they've already talked to, what the committee or buyer already knows about your organization, and why they've contacted you last. Then resell the value you offer and the results you can bring to the table. Finally, be confident. Hold your ground on your standard pricing and terms.

TIP 306: *Add or Subtract in Small Increments*

Never make large jumps. Large concessions indicate to your buyers that your opening price was probably too high. That in itself creates distrust and costs you credibility—something you can't afford to lose at any time in the sales relationship, but particularly at this point in price discussions.

Making same-size concessions—in other words, to continue lowering your price by 10 percent on each counteroffer—tempts the buyers to keep asking for more and more discounts, changes, and options.

Smaller and smaller concessions, on the other hand, signal to your buyers that you're being squeezed to the limit on your price point—that you're at the walk-away point. Their conclusion? If they want to do business, they'd better make a decision and stop pushing before they have to start over at ground zero with another supplier.

TIP 307: *Make "Split the Difference" Work for You*

Why isn't splitting the difference always a good idea? Buyers may know your price all through the sales cycle, and then when you're ready to close the deal, they say they expect you to do the project for X amount or that you'll have to match the price of the incumbent vendor at Y dollars. The buyers then are expecting you to counter with an "Okay, let's split the difference" compromise.

The original counteroffer, though, may be too low in the first place. You can be led into conceding a price that is much lower than you intended. Finally, you may set a precedent for all negotiations with that buyer of "splitting the difference."

Of course, if this idea works in your favor, agree and you'll both walk away thinking you have a good deal.

TIP 308: *Find Your Buyers' Benchmark*

When buyers ask you to discount with some vague statement such as "You'll need to do better than that," then you'll need to uncover the expectations with a specific question. Ask the buyers for the basis for their judgment that the price is too high: Are they comparing the price to what they paid last year? To what they hoped the price would be? To what they paid for the service ten years ago? To what a colleague in another organization thought it should be?

With this insight, you can begin to reset their expectation and educate the buyers about how the price truly compares to the industry or how you set prices in general. Once you understand the basis of the comment that "your price is too high," then you will better know how to proceed—whether to negotiate, justify, or simply educate your buyers. (Also see tips in Chapter 4 under "Concerns about Pricing.")

TIP 309: *State Ranges, Not Specifics, in Making Concessions*

When your buyers ask you to make a trade, such as to lower the price in exchange for placing a bigger order or to give a discount if their own organization handles a certain phase of the project, then state your counteroffer within a range.

Examples: "If you could order as many as 2,000 units at one time, we could save start-up costs, and I could probably give you a 10 to 15 percent discount on that kind of volume." "If your own people want to handle the information-collection phase of the project before we take over, I could refigure my cost. My guess is that would save somewhere between 6 and 9 percent of the total project price."

The goal is to learn more information about your buyer's situation and expectations before you agree to a definite price.

TIP 310: *Attach a Value to the Add-Ons*

If you've agreed to provide add-ons at no charge, be sure the buyers know what clients typically pay for those add-ons. Also let the buyers know your cost to your own supplier. Buyers can't and don't value what they don't understand.

TIP 311: *Play the Role of Reluctant Seller*

Of course, your buyers know you want to make the sale, but "how badly" is the issue. Your objective is to make the sale at the price stated. After all, what salesperson is eager to give up profit margins and commissions?

Never reconsider "on the spot" and lower your price quickly; otherwise, buyers will always think they could have gotten a better deal. You always can defer to a higher authority to make the decision, or explain that you have to have time to review your numbers or check with your suppliers or give some thought to where you could cut your own costs to deliver.

Then leave the door open for a trade or counteroffer.

TIP 312: *Understand How the Phone Changes Negotiation Issues*

Generally, high-ticket negotiations take place face to face and sensitive, difficult issues get hammered out toes to toes. Loose ends can be tied up over the phone, but sometimes the minor telephone "logistical afterthoughts" may not be afterthoughts at all. Buyers may purposely bring up sensitive issues later, thinking that you will be more likely to concede on these points rather than unravel a "done deal." Often, they word their request as a casual, "Oh, just one more thing. . . ."

It can be tempting to agree to such requests. You're in a good frame of mind because you've just made the sale, and you don't want to risk upsetting your buyers by refusing them. Besides, the chances are that by doing this "one more little thing," you'll be able to cement your relationship and win future opportunities.

Consider such items as part of the overall package—not just a logistical detail of delivery and execution.

TIP 313: *Treat Nibblers As You Would Gobblers*

The problem is that this "one small thing"—whether it's free delivery, extended payment terms, or technical support—can drastically alter your profit picture.

After you've arrived at an agreement, you have several responses to stop the buyers' nibbling before your cheese is all gone. As always, the best option is prevention; that is, make buyers feel good about the sale— make them feel they've already won the best deal possible. If they attempt to nibble, show buyers the cost of add-ons. They may not be aware of how much you typically charge for things like training, shipping, an extended warranty, or a carrying case.

If at the last minute, when you've come to a total package price, the buyers start to ask for freebies or to subtract options, and along with it your built-in profit margin, point out that cuts in options may decrease the results to be gained with your solution.

Another way to stop nibbling is to raise the potential that you'll have to start the negotiation all over. Say: "I thought we were in agreement on that point. Maybe we need to go over these issues again to verify what we can and can't include." If buyers feel they've gotten a good deal to that point, they'll hesitate before taking a chance on unraveling the whole negotiated arrangement.

A final strategy is to reverse the nibble. Ask the buyer to increase the order size, upgrade the model, or handle the installation with internal staff to "balance" the "trade-off." Either you profit, too, from the change in the agreement or the buyer stops nibbling.

TIP 314: *Beware of a Counteroffer That's Too High*

If your buyer has asked for a trade on price and your counteroffer remains too high, you risk several things: Your buyer may lose patience and walk away, thinking you'll never get together; the competition may undercut you and take the business; or you may feel forced to make a final, drastic drop in price to save the sale, thus losing credibility.

These dangers particularly surface in difficult negotiations with teams of buyers and myriad of competitors.

TIP 315: *Negotiate Packages, Not Points*

Asking the buyers to state all goals up front and mentioning everything you'd like to have in trade is far more effective than agreeing to things on a point-by-point basis.

First, having all the options on the table up front saves time because no hidden agendas or last-minute surprises crop up. Contrarily, when you're negotiating point by point, you'll find that you continually have to return to readdress earlier issues. Second, with more options and issues on the table, you can be more flexible when buyers ask you to make concessions and toss in this or that for free.

The goal is to put together a complete package—the buyer's investment in exchange for your solution that delivers results.

TIP 316: *Be the One to Write the Contract*

Typically, the seller handles the paperwork, though not always. Sometimes when you're selling to a large organization, the buyer's organization prefers to have its own legal department draw up contracts and finalize the Statement of Work to correspond to its Request for Proposal. Be sure to take every opportunity to do the paperwork. If you can't or don't want to draft the entire document, at least offer to draft the troublesome or complex clauses for insertion in the buyer's contract.

Although a little extra work on your part, drafting the contract gives you several advantages: First, the document should be more comprehensive because you've taken notes throughout the discussion about what your buyer wants and needs and what you have and have *not* offered to do. Also, because you know your product and service better than your buyer, you can use the appropriate terminology and refer to issues and terms specifically rather than vaguely.

In addition, you may discover later that you've forgotten to discuss certain issues with your buyer, or vice versa, and the buyer may have questions or issues that never came up earlier. If you draft the agreement, you'll have opportunity to add those in the way you want them to read. You'll also have opportunity to reframe positively any sensitive issues that were finally hammered out in your discussions.

Never look upon this as an opportunity to "put one over" on your buyer by slipping in extra items. You want the final written agreement to soothe buyers, not upset them all over again or raise new problems and reopen the negotiation.

TIP 317: *Sweeten the Deal*

Think of your buyers as your guests. When guests ring your doorbell, you typically answer the door to greet them, ask them to have a seat or step inside for a few moments, offer them food or drink, and tell them to make themselves comfortable. If they stay long enough, you try to find something to entertain them.

The same courtesies apply to buyers during a negotiation. Be gracious enough to offer something such as a small gift (of course, nothing valuable enough to be considered a bribe); a dinner or lunch; your undivided attention to their family or a hobby; or concede a point to their opinion on an issue. Thoughtfulness in any of these ways pays dividends. It makes the other people feel as though they should reciprocate in some way, and they often do—with concessions and referrals.

Charging a fair, reasonable price for your product or service—instead of a discounted one—also allows you to "give something back to the buyer" in more substantial ways. You are able to sweeten the deal by throwing in something extra—like free shipping or extra training time—without damaging your profit.

Both you and the buyers walk away from such sales feeling as though you've each won.

TIP 318: *Negotiate the Entire Deal Before You Deliver—Always*

It's understandable why salespeople let themselves get dragged into starting a project before "all the details get worked out and the paperwork signed." After all, it's the honeymoon period. Everyone's in a good mood. Trust is high. You don't want to do anything to upset the buyer while the deal's in a precarious position and before the ink's dry.

What sometimes happens, though, is that a product is delivered, used, consumed, or damaged before the buyer pays for it. The same is true for services, and once those services are performed, there's little recourse for the seller. The perceived—and real—value drops dramatically in the buyer's eyes.

What started out as a high-potential partnership deteriorates into a haggle over payment.

6

DEALING WITH
DIFFICULT BUYERS

If not for these difficult situations with prospects and buyers, sales professionals would pay their organizations to let them come to work every day. These are the times and types that try men's and women's souls. Or has that already been said? Never mind, it's still true. So anticipate and develop your responses and techniques to handle each situation with finesse and success.

THE RECLUSE

Recluses hide behind their gatekeepers and their voicemail. If your Recluse is a prospect, you may question whether they actually need your solution and have authority to buy. If not, wait until the Recluse reappears in the appropriate buying stage.

The more frustrating experience, however, is having a Recluse for a client—someone who has already signed on the dotted line but with whom you need to interact to implement the sale or service the account.

TIP 319: *Send E-mail or Letters*

Recluses generally respond—at their leisure. No matter how busy and what the crisis brewing, communicate with written correspondence via e-mail or letters. Recluses can read your full message without interruption, even if at midnight. A written message allows Recluses total control over their time and the interaction, something they demand from all who do business with them.

TIP 320: *Leave Complete, Concise Voicemails That Specify Action*

Avoid leaving Recluse prospects "teaser" voicemails that aim to elicit callbacks. Leave two or, at most, three voicemails, spread over a couple of months that answer this question very specifically and succinctly: Why should they return your call? What specific value can you give them immediately—a demo, an answer to a question, needed research?

If you're calling a client, specify the action you want, supply all the details they need to take action, and don't necessarily ask for a call back. Instead, give clients options to reply. Ten to one, they'll reply by e-mail so they can control the length of the interaction and respond on their own schedule.

TIP 321: *Hook a Funny Bone*

If you've left several messages with a prospect or buyer, or written a couple of times and received no response, you may want to try a humorous "checklist" sent by e-mail or regular mail. If your Recluse has a sense of humor, this often breaks the ice and generates a call back or a more elaborate e-mail response that answers your real, earlier messages.

Mr. Recluse:

I've tried several times but have been unable to reach you. Please check your response below:

___We're in crisis mode. We're all bleeding. Call 911.

___ I'm working under a hectic deadline. Call me back in _____ days.

___ I'm asking _____ to handle this for me. You can reach her/him at _____ and I'll let him/her know to expect a contact from you.

___ I got your earlier voice mails, and I did it already!

___ I'm really a nice person. I just don't like to talk on the phone. Please send me your literature, telling me all about it. I promise to take a look.

___ Go away. You've got the right person, but I have no interest, none, nada, zip, zero.

___ Do you want be to call my friend Guido?

Most will have a sense of humor and respond. Some will not have a sense of humor—but will be ashamed to admit this deficiency. They'll get the point, however, and move the action along because they do want to implement your solution or take a look at your offer.

TIP 322: *Connect on a Personal Interest*

Show a broader interest in Recluses than just what you can sell them. Forward a brochure on a trade show they might be interested in attending—one that your organization *won't* be attending but that they might have interest in. Send something related to a Recluse's hobby, hometown, health club, or children's school.

TIP 323: *Grab Attention with Something Unique to Your Product or Service*

If you're a marketing company, send a singing telegram with your latest successful TV jingle. If you sell candy, send a candy gram. If you rep for a clothing manufacturer, put your message or slogan on a t-shirt and pay teenagers to stand outside the elevator in the lobby of your Recluse's building. If you sell courier service, offer complimentary delivery of your Recluse's Christmas packages next year.

TIP 324: *Find Another Door*

Casually try to meet others in the organization (such as at trade shows or at monthly association meetings) and mention to them that you're trying to "work with Ms. Recluse" on a project and ask for "advice" on her personal work style and schedule as you move through the implementation process. Often, they can share names of others in the organization who may be able to provide you with the information needed to move the process along so that you can bypass your contact on minor issues.

TIP 325: *Don't Become Entangled in Your Ego*

Sometimes locking horns with a Recluse becomes a challenge of the wills. When it does, you lose.

While I was working from my home office on a book for a few weeks, I received a call from someone about midmorning, asking for my husband by name. I told him my husband wasn't home. The caller said he'd try again later. The next day he called back about the same time. I again told him my husband wasn't available. On this second call, he identified his organization, stating that he was calling about "investment opportunities" and said he'd try again later. (I'm always a little intrigued by such callers who never bother to clarify who makes the investment decisions for the family, which happens to be me in our case.)

A few days later, the same broker called back at 6:30 AM, asking for my husband again. Although he didn't give his name, I recognized the voice. When I told him my husband wasn't there (he had gone to the office early that morning), the broker got really rude and slammed down the receiver. Now the war was on. He called every few days for months, night and day, determined to catch my husband answering the phone himself. I was just as determined that he not catch him.

First, there was no need. Our investments were being handled well with another firm. Second, the caller acted like a jerk. He had let his ego get the better of his judgment—and his time.

In this case, the Recluse was in actuality no Recluse. Know when to move on.

THE HOSTILE HOSTAGE

Hostile Hostages have been forced to buy from you against their will. Either their boss has made the decision to buy from you and left them only the formalities of signing the contract, or they served on a decision-making team and cast a dissenting vote against you as supplier. Subsequently, they have been selected to administer the contract and serve as the point of contact.

You also run into Hostile Hostages when you're a sole-source provider—you're the only kid on the block with the toy the customer wants or needs.

TIP 326: *Don't "Pull Rank" If You Came In up the Food Chain*

If you made your connection and, in effect, the sale to the Hostile Hostage's boss, never tout that situation. Your Hostile Hostage knows that all too well. Set your goal on winning the confidence and trust of your current contact. Eliminate comments such as "When Mr. VIP and I spoke the other day, we were discussing the importance of . . ." or "Ms. VIP wanted me to let you know that . . ." Such comments convey that you're on the inside track and your buyer is the outsider in his or her own backyard.

Your buyer will work to lower the rungs on your ladder.

TIP 327: *Never Assume You Can Quit Selling*

Just because the boss "made the decision," don't automatically assume that the decision can't or won't be reversed. Assume that you must also establish your personal credibility with the Hostile Hostage and the credibility of your product or service and organization. Although you may not make other formal presentations, look for opportunities to drop credentials and evidence of performance into your conversations. Every contact, particularly your primary buyer and liaison, needs confidence that you can deliver the solution you've promised.

TIP 328: *Make the Buyer a Star*

Never leave your Hostile Hostages in the dark about what kind of press they're getting when you're alone with the boss. Copy the boss on e-mails of commendation about how they're handling the implementation and the relationship. Make sure your oral comments to the boss get "filtered" back down to the Hostage.

Make Hostile Hostages stars in your story and let them know it.

THE POWERLESS POTENTATE

Powerless Potentates refuse to admit they have no real authority to buy. They serve as recommenders, influencers, and gatekeepers—but never the final decision maker. The only reason they become "difficult" in the selling process is that their refusal to admit lack of authority keeps you from reaching the decision maker effectively with your story. Powerless Potentates do not always act from egocentric motivation—sometimes they hesitate to admit they have no authority for fear you will not negotiate with them when their boss sends them out to seek favors.

TIP 329: *Consider Carefully before Going over This Person's Head*

Ask yourself these questions: How do I know the boss will respond any differently? Who likely set up the arrangement? What do I have to gain? What do I have to lose?

TIP 330: *Lead the Powerless Potentate to Admit the Situation*

You will become suspicious about these buyers' authority when they always have time to return your calls and meet with you, but are always fuzzy about when they'll have a decision.

When your gut begins to tell you that you may be dealing with a Powerless Potentate, start asking questions, a few at a time, until you lead the person to admit the truth. Here are some starter questions: "How do you go about setting your budget for these sorts of items?" "Do your managers have input to your budget, or do you set the budget figures yourself?" "Are you on a zero-based budget system, or just exactly how do you go about doing your planning?" "What kind of difficulties do you typically have in deciding on budget issues year after year?" "Do you have to haggle with other departments over allocated funds? For example, if you get your requested budget, does that mean they don't get their funds?" "How involved are the procedures you have to go through if you decide you need to go back to the drawing board, so to speak—if you decide you need to request additional funds for a special pet project?" "Are you the only one with the authority to make requests for budget alterations or to approve expenditures in your functional area?"

You get the picture. They either can or can't answer the questions. They'll either be comfortable or ill at ease with such questions. They'll either be informative or evasive. In any case, it will become evident that the person is too unknowledgeable to be the real decision maker.

Then, once the Powerless Potentate admits that fact, you can move forward in the sales cycle. Start by enlisting the influencer's help as your sponsor to sell to the real decision maker.

TIP 331: *Become a Coach*

Provide your Powerless Potentates with all the information and help they need to present you well to their boss or team. Ask them to brief you on the current problems, what has worked well, what has not worked at all, what goofs past suppliers have made, and what new criteria have been established as a result.

Suggest surveys. Suggest interviews and meetings they might arrange for you. Ask them to introduce you to other divisions to gather data and brainstorm from the ground floor up before you put together a proposal for the boss. Next, put together a proposal and coach them on how to prepare the boss for your call. You also could suggest when and how to arrange a team meeting and at what point you should present your formal proposal.

Assure them that you will deliver value to their boss and the organization, and that you will make them look good for having discovered you as a resource.

TIP 332: *Put It in Writing*

If the Powerless Potentate still cannot be convinced to let you meet with the real decision maker, put your story in writing—with a succinct, high-impact overview. No matter how ineffective the gatekeeper, it will be difficult for this person to destroy your persuasive message in print.

TIP 333: *Create a Crisis at an Opportune Time*

Plant a seed that you have a "breakthrough" idea or valuable information to share with the decision maker that "may become available at any time." Explain that you'll be in touch just as soon as possible because you want to give their organization the earliest notice possible. (This "breakthrough" information might be survey results from your organization, release of a new product, publication of a white paper, award of a patent, new pricing discounts, or announcement of a new strategic partnership.)

Then look for the Powerless Potentate's first absence—a holiday, sickness, vacation, travel out of the country. Leave them a voicemail, explaining that you need to get in touch right away. When they don't return the call immediately, escalate the issue or news to the boss or team—the real decision maker(s)—and use that "breakthrough idea/information" as your introduction and opportunity.

After the interaction with the boss or the team, phone or e-mail your Powerless Potentate again, explaining who you contacted in their absence and why the issue was such an opportunity that couldn't wait until their return.

Assume others in the organization will appreciate the fact that you've been concerned with the welfare of the entire organization—not just the ego of the individual buyer.

THE STALLER

Stallers typically suffer from indecisiveness. They may or may not be a powerless tiger or political misfit, but the result to you proves to be the same: meeting after meeting; phone conversation after conversation;

request after request for more information, proposals, pricing break-downs, references, and evidence of results—and still no decision.

TIP 334: *Ask Yourself "Why the Indecision?"*

Buyers may stall at the point of decision for any number of reasons. Your response, of course, will depend on the reason:

- They can't decide about the product or service. (Response: Offer more evidence and proof.)
- They can't decide about you or your organization. (Response: Increase credibility.)
- They can't determine how the decision might go over inside a "down" internal climate. (Response: Help them gather input or show value in a negative climate.)
- They are posturing for a price discount. (Response: Wait.)
- The answer is no and they're too timid to tell you. (Response: Ask point blank and give them permission to be straightforward with you.)

TIP 335: *Offer Guarantees*

Create opportunities for the indecisive to touch, see, feel, and experience your product or service. Provide all the possible evidence of results. Put the indecisive in touch with references who can offer assurances. Delay payment options until the buyer has opportunity to "sample" your service and trust that you will not deliver and then run and hide.

TIP 336: *Help the Indecisive to Pass the Buck*

Once you determine Stallers incapable of making a decision no matter what guarantees you offer, help them to pass the decision off to others—for example, their boss, a team of colleagues such as a task force, or even a subordinate "who needs to develop judgment skills in making such a decision." If the would-be target is a task force, volunteer to help get the group organized.

Yes, generally, it's tougher to sell to a committee, but you still have a better chance of selling to an action-oriented committee than a stalled individual.

TIP 337: *Create Deadlines or Incentives to Buy*

People have become accustomed to acting under pressure and re-acting in crisis. It may be that your buyers cannot decide until there's a deadline. If this is the case, create a discount that's good only until X date. Offer a bonus that's good for only Y weeks. Mention the benefit of seeing a demonstration and enrolling in X training for 50 managers— but only if a contract is signed in time to make the demo and training arrangements by Z date.

TIP 338: *Decrease the Frequency but Increase the Volume*

Decisions demand emotional energy for Stallers. To remove the pain, decrease the number of buying decisions the individual has to make: Decrease the order frequency while you increase the order volume so that the person has to order from you only one time per year instead of once a quarter.

TIP 339: *Limit Choices to the Important Few Instead of the Meaningless Many*

Don't let trivial decisions overwhelm Stallers' overloaded circuits so that they're tempted to pull the plug on the whole buying situation. Arrange all the details of your most popular choices into Plan A, Plan B, and Plan C choices. Offer those options as packages so Stallers don't have to tackle them step by step, decision by decision.

TIP 340: *Write Contracts with Automatic Renewals*

Allow Stallers to make as few decisions as possible. For example, propose a multiyear contract. You then can add automatic renewal clauses that require no action from the Staller to remain in force unless you opt to raise your prices.

TIP 341: *Rev Your Engine Before You Get to the Intersection*

Don't wait until you need a decision to ask for one. Start early and assume that the Staller will renew an expiring contract, mentioning new value you'll be offering under the new arrangements. Waiting until a few days before you need to get a buyer signed on the dotted line is like pulling out into the middle of the intersection and then stopping to wait for the signal light to change. Chances are likely you'll get hit before that happens.

Stallers need time to adjust to any change.

THE TYRANT

Tyrants behave aggressively. They are abrasive and often lie to get what they want. Their mission is to win concessions; their method, intimidation.

TIP 342: *Never Assume Tyrants Are a Solo Act*

A salesperson's typical first reaction is this: If only the Tyrant's boss knew what a jerk is representing the organization! Sometimes the sales agent goes over the Tyrant's head to discuss the issue with the next level of management—only to be disappointed with the reception. They discover that the boss is applauding the results the Tyrant achieves by such aggressive intimidation of salespeople.

TIP 343: *Moan and Groan, but Don't Bleed*

Tyrants are typically purchasing agents. It's their job to squeeze you to your limits—to extract every ounce of wiggle room in the profit margin. It's your job to hold firm. If they squeeze and you moan and groan loudly enough, you've made them look good just for roughing you up. You don't necessarily have to bleed price concessions for Tyrants to get credit and become heroes in their organization.

TIP 344: *Play Powerless*

With a Tyrant who keeps pushing for concessions, let your boss or other executives be the bad guys. In general, using the absent decision maker is always a good negotiating tactic, but particularly effective when the Tyrant continues to push for things you cannot grant. Never, however, agree that your management "should" grant such things because it presents your organization in a bad light and damages credibility.

TIP 345: *Call the Tyrant to Repeat and Confirm or Deny an Insult*

Rather than hear your buyer insult you or your organization and just let it pass, question it point blank: "Do you really mean what you just said—you think that I/we . . ." and then paraphrase the insult. Examples: "Are you actually saying you think my organization has been artificially manipulating the supply of widgets to affect pricing?" "In your last e-mail you implied that our management had been engaged in manufacturing and inspection improprieties. Is that the position of your organization or your personal opinion?"

Often, the person will start backpedaling and say you misunderstood and that's not what he or she meant and modify the comment. But you will have accomplished your mission—to convey the message that the Tyrant has expressed a direct insult and that you understood it well.

The implied message is that you will need to consider that comment carefully in any future interactions to determine if you want to do business with the buyer's organization. For buyers who need you as a supplier, the effect will not be lost.

TIP 346: *Use a Matter-of-Fact Tone and Move On*

When the Tyrant demands something, hold your ground. State what you can and can't do in a matter-of-fact tone and with matter-of-fact phrasing. Keep your cool. Instead of pausing and holding eye contact as if you're expecting a reaction and argument, break eye contact. Assume you're ready to move on to the next topic of discussion.

TIP 347: *Repeat the Sound Track*

Repeat what you can and can't do, over and over and over and over. The Tyrant uses emotion to create uncomfortable reactions. You foil their intimidating manner by remaining unruffled.

TIP 348: *Let 'Em See You Sweat*

If the calm, cool, and collected response doesn't work with your Tyrant, don't hesitate to let the buyer know that you feel under pressure because you've given the very best deal you can. Then ask for a definite commitment to buy. Tyrants are looking for physical evidence that they have received your very best deal.

TIP 349: *Use Silence to Diffuse and Focus the Tyrant*

When a yelling and cursing customer calls you as the "project manager" of the sale, try silence—complete silence as you listen. Eventually, the Tyrant will wind down and ask: "Are you there?" Then you can respond: "Yes, I'm here, but I'm going to need you to work with me and focus on the problem to get it resolved."

If they continue to curse and yell, buy some time to let them cool down by asking them to hold on "while you check their records," "while you get on the other line to check with the service people," or "while you call someone to get information and then call them back with all the facts in ten minutes." This brief "time out" allows the Tyrant to cool off and stop shouting long enough to allow you to guide the discussion in more productive ways.

TIP 350: *Acknowledge and State a Different Perspective*

Listen to and acknowledge the Tyrant's viewpoint. Then state your own, different perspective in a matter-of-fact manner: "I understand what you're saying, but I see the situation a little differently. Here's my take on the situation and what I think we can do under the circumstances. . . ."

THE INCOMPETENT

Incompetents can't be labeled that way simply because they aren't smart enough to buy from you. In fact, the Incompetent may even be a positive individual—someone simply new to the job, not yet familiar with the industry and product—receptive to your message and open to building a strong relationship with you and your organization. But Incompetent buyers, whatever the cause, generally require time and special handling.

TIP 351: *Give Them a "YOU ARE HERE" Presentation*

If you discover that they're lost in knowing how to buy your product and don't know how to make apples-to-apples comparisons, give Incompetents a map—an educational presentation on how to buy. As part of your sales presentation, tell them what they should look for in features, benefits, results, suppliers, quality, and pricing.

More experienced buyers in their position will already know these things, but less experienced buyers will need a map to help them find their way to you.

TIP 352: *Win Their Loyalty First*

Incompetents typically get and keep their jobs because "they know somebody." It just stands to reason that relationships are primary to them. So get to know them, establish trust, and then sell to them on the basis of that relationship.

TIP 353: *Draw Boundary Lines and Tell Them When to Step in and Out*

Incompetent buyers sometimes ask you to do things that even your very best customers wouldn't dare ask, and then fail to ask for commitments and discounts they're entitled to have!

Put aside the assumptions you make about other professional buyers and have a heart-to-heart chat with these Incompetents without fear that you'll offend. When they ask you to jump over the moon, assume they don't know what they're asking. Don't explode—just explain. "We can't alter X because . . . , but here's what I can do for you. . . ." Likewise when they place a volume order, explain that they're entitled to X, Y, Z with that size order.

There is no need to bring up these issues in front of their boss or team, and no need to "put it in writing" in an e-mail. Just draw the lines in the dirt and let the buyer know what's the acceptable norm and what's out of line.

TIP 354: *Show Them the Ropes in Their Own Organization*

Many times Incompetent buyers are also Incompetent employees in general. Not only do they not know how to buy from you, neither do they know how things get done in their own organization.

For example, if their approval limit rests at $10,000 and your product costs $12,000, do they understand that you may have to submit two invoices—one for the product at $10,000 and one for the maintenance agreement and supplies at $2,000? Or, if they need input from the branch managers and can't get consensus, subtly drop hints on how their predecessor used the "do it, then ask forgiveness" principle to gain compliance from the field.

TIP 355: *Create a Path of Least Resistance*

The mantra of Incompetents is to "stay off the radar screen." Translated, that means that once they announce a decision, they don't want to "undecide." Once they justify price to their peers or the purchasing people, they don't want to have to re-explain it and get approval from the boss for a new supplier.

Be sure to design your offer with the long-term contract in mind. The bad news: You'll need to live with the pricing and terms for a long time. The good news: It will be hard to unseat you as an incumbent.

TIP 356: *Lead with a Shorter Arm*

More experienced buyers enjoy more latitude and more choices in their buying decisions. They frequently do not care what "everybody else is doing." Less competent buyers need a stronger guide through the buying process, who may need to prevent confusion by limiting their choices: "I think Model Z, not Model X, will be more appropriate for your shop here. Did you want to shoot for delivery during first quarter?"

When Incompetents wander to inappropriate choices, reign them in with helpful hints: "Our smartest clients really appreciate the way X works." "Inexperienced buyers never seem to think about Y, but that can cause problems in situations where climate control is an issue."

Incompetents listen to a strong leader.

TIP 357: *Continue to Evaluate the Trade-Off of Time versus Profitability*

You can help Incompetents for hours and years before they buy—or they may *never* buy—your product or service. Continually evaluate your time spent hand-holding to measure your return on investment.

TIP 358: *Charge Consulting Time*

As a last resort, you may find Incompetents asking you to spend so much time with them that you're doing their job for them. At first, they call you with a few questions about your product or service. Next, they call you with general questions about issues or problems, and you look for selling opportunities. Yet time and time again, you realize they pick your brain to solve a problem without buying your product or services. Eventually, they are using you as their personal consultant—and your only fee is hope of future business.

The first step may be to limit these calls with a comment such as: "Sure, I'd be happy to spend about ten minutes with you on the phone before I leave for another appointment. How can I help?"

In response to their requests for mysterious meetings, you might probe with: "Can you give me a little more insight about the agenda— who'll be in the meeting? Exactly what's our goal?" Such questions put these buyers on the spot to have a goal and at least go through the motions of discussing selling opportunities. If that doesn't happen, you'll be prepared for the next such request.

Finally, you may want to take the last step, with a gentle suggestion: "I'm unclear about the exact purpose of our meeting. It seems as though we're moving into more of a consulting relationship. If that's your interest, I'd be happy to quote you our rates for that and set up some time later in the week. Just let me make sure I'm the correct person to help you with those issues. If you tell me what exactly it is that you wanted help with, I'll know if I should quote you my consulting rates, or put you in touch with one of our technical staff."

A straightforward approach will set the record straight. A buyer may truly need the help and feel guilty about taking your time while not buying, and yet not know that your organization provides consulting services at a fee. In that case, clear communication works well for both you and the Incompetent.

THE KNOW-IT-ALL

Some Know-It-Alls really do have superior expertise; others do not. They're pseudoexperts who assume the posture and position of the true expert. In either case, their tone of superiority and ego dictates that you approach Know-It-Alls in a different manner.

TIP 359: *Steer Clear of the Stereotypical View of a "Sales Presentation"*

If anyone ever had a basic built-in resistance to a sales presentation, Know-It-Alls do. They consider themselves much too bright to sit and listen to someone do a canned sales presentation, complete with a formal Q&A. So steer clear of these and instead aim for a fresh dialogue.

TIP 360: *Do Your Homework*

Start your sales call on a discussion of the footnotes rather than the thesis statement. You cannot "wing it" with Know-It-Alls. Do some extra research—above what you'd ordinarily do on prospective clients—and make sure you understand the industry and their business issues.

TIP 361: *Open the Door with New Data, Information, or Ideas*

Brilliant people got that way most often by reading and listening. Experts can chew on intriguing tidbits of information or ideas for hours. Be the conduit for news—recent survey results, newly published conclusions about an industry issue, or a technical puzzle to be solved and a potential solution that you'd like to test in their organization—in exchange for their listening to your entire story.

TIP 362: *Respect Their Expertise Rather Than Compete with It*

Know-It-Alls have spent years accumulating a wealth of information and expertise, and the know-it-all attitude tells you that they're proud of it. You may win an argument—but never a sale—by matching wits. Instead, without diminishing your own expertise, permit Know-It-Alls to share their know-how and bask in the spotlight. Ask questions that allow them to showcase their knowledge and acknowledge any experiences they put on display.

TIP 363: *Prime the Pump with Questions*

Know-It-Alls love to talk. Move the sales conversation along with questions for Know-It-Alls to reveal hidden opportunities where your product or service can help solve their problems. Instead of jumping in to tell them how your solution can help, ask questions and let them tell *you:* How much money and time do they estimate the current problem is costing them? What's the best way and fastest way to implement your solution and get others on board?

Know-It-Alls believe their own data, so let them talk and sell themselves.

TIP 364: *Never Contradict; Just Offer an "Alternative"*

Know-It-Alls do not want to lose face by being wrong. Therefore, as you recommend, choose your words carefully so that they have two right choices. Examples: "*Another approach* for someone in your situation—one that might make sense for someone in your shoes—is to do X." "*Another viewpoint* on this issue would be to make this a two-phase installation project. We could. . . ." "Here's *another way* to look at the value of this approach. . . ." "Well, you've outlined *one approach* and *one philosophy,* certainly. Here's *another view* some clients express. . . ." "Of course, what you mention is a sensible approach. Sound reasoning. An *alternative plan*—I'll call it Plan Two—would be to order. . . ."

Give them time to think over the options privately and then come back to you with *their* choice and an explanation about why your suggestion has been their idea all along.

TIP 365: *Give Them an Idea to Modify and Claim*

Know-It-Alls cannot bear the thought of acting on other people's ideas. Therefore, treat them as consultants. Give them raw data collected from their organization that would "imply" they need help. Next, take them a "rough idea" of what you could offer that "might fit" their situation. "Toss out" some suggestions and ask for their "suggestions" and "help" in "formulating a plan of action" that "might have value" for them.

Sit back and watch as the Know-It-All creates the solution you can bring back in proposal form during the next meeting to propose to their entire team. Be sure to give your Know-It-All full credit for devising the solution and let them help you sell it to the group.

TIP 366: *Blind Yourself to Their Arrogance and Build a Friendship*

Arrogant people make enemies, not friends. An inroad to winning their business may be to offer your friendship first.

THE WHINER

Whiners are never pleased with your organization. Nothing is right. Whiners are convinced that your executive team, the dock workers, and the technicians stay up nights trying to figure out how to deceive them and ruin their operations. What's more, they expect you to take their side against your own organization!

TIP 367: *Never Agree with the Whiner and Focus on Your Organization's Weaknesses*

Sales professionals occasionally take this tact when Whiners begin to complain about their product's or organization's weaknesses because they think that agreement and empathy will build the relationship, which, in turn, will help them make the sale. If you're of this mind-set, please reconsider. Relentless complaining and commiserating about what your organization will or won't do for its clients, the pricing discounts it will or won't give, or the service it delivers or fails to deliver during implementation, devalues your product. Why would that lead you closer to a sale?

TIP 368: *Consider Whining as Posturing to Negotiate*

When a prospect begins to complain about this or that product or service limitation, be warned. Often such pre-buy talk is an attempt to put you on the defensive and prepare you to offer a concession to "make up for" the perceived deficiency.

Seasoned negotiators frequently take this whining tact: "Your home office must be totally out of touch with reality. No way is that financing policy acceptable in today's environment. When's the last time one of your corporate suits talked to a real client?"

Expect this posturing, and understand its purpose.

TIP 369: *Give More Personal Positive Attention*

Negative attention can be better than no attention at all. Sometimes Whiners feel that no one pays attention unless they grumble. (Unfortunately, that may be true. After all "the squeaky wheel gets the grease" became a cliché for good reason.) Show these clients more positive attention and see if the whining decreases.

TIP 370: *Try Humor*

Some clients enjoy misery, and they love company with their misery. When you know your clients well enough to understand that whining is a personality trait, try humor. Play "ain't it awful" with the appropriate body language and matching sad stories with a light twist. (Just make sure not to join the whining about your own organization, as noted in Tip 367.)

TIP 371: *Consider the Complaint a Preventive Measure*

Whiners sometimes complain about every past sale and every little thing that has gone wrong to date in the current sales cycle ("No one called from EG to verify color like you said they would." "Are you sure this code is correct—you said you'd call after you checked the newer catalog and you didn't call."), simply because they fear a foul-up with their order. They see complaining as a way to keep you on top of the details of the situation. Their motto: Complain before there's a foul-up so there won't be a foul-up.

TIP 372: *Use Your Whiner as an Intelligence Source*

Redirect your Whiner's focus from your own organization to the Whiner's own company or to a competitor. Ask a few questions to get the Whiner off and running and you'll learn how someone in a buying position sees your competitors, who's putting pressure on the Whiner to do what, who the influencers are, and what could turn the situation around.

Examples: "You've been pointing out some of our own service difficulties—tell me, are others in the industry experiencing the same issues?" "Do other buyers in your organization feel the same way you do about these manufacturing specs?" "Are others in your division aiming for the same quality standards as you have mind, or are they more concerned with meeting your target installation date and then working out any bugs in the system later?"

Whiners can be a major source of valuable information to you if you know how to focus them tactfully.

TIP 373: *Collect and Share the Positive Buzz*

If your organization has positive PR going already, all you need to do is to collect it and pass it along to your Whiners in periodic chunks. Send them industry articles about you, quotes from your executives in the press, and brochures mentioning presentations at industry meetings by your company representatives.

If such buzz hasn't been started, you'll need to build it yourself. Use a clipping service to find articles about your organization or search the Internet. Print out chat room conversations that show your performance in a favorable light. Pull together testimonial letters written to headquarters from your strategic partners. Ask your favorite clients for testimonials. Do a client survey and then summarize the results to your Whiners.

Build the buzz. Collect the buzz. Share the buzz. Be the buzz.

TIP 374: *Be the Face on Your Whole Company*

Obviously, Whiners like you personally or you wouldn't be "in the know" about the other "deficient" people, products, policies, and procedures at your organization. If your prospects fear the way others at your company may handle their business, promise to handle the implementation and coordination details yourself. In short, become a one-person company for that client.

When you can't possibly handle all the details yourself, at least be the go-between. Make a special effort to introduce the Whiner to a key executive or a key support person so that, when you're unavailable, that individual becomes the "face" of the company.

TIP 375: *Offer to Pass on a Complaint to the "Powers That Be"*

If Whiners continue to complain, probe to find out how serious the issue is by suggesting that they put their complaint in writing so that you can pass it on to your executive team for consideration. Granted, that's more work than complaining aloud to you face to face—and that's the point. Your offer in effect says "put up or shut up."

TIP 376: *Ask for a Commitment If You Resolve the Issue*

If Whiners use their complaints as reasons not to buy or reasons to stop doing business with your organization, ask if they would be willing to commit to the purchase or a continued relationship if you can resolve the issues they're complaining about. If they say yes, write the issues down in their presence. Now you have your plan of action.

TIP 377: *Focus on the Product, Not Your Organization*

If Whiners cannot be satisfied with your organization, direct their focus to the product itself. You have a great solution to their problem. So focus them on their vision of value for the future. Make your organization "beside the point."

TIP 378: *Ask to Be Left out of Uncomfortable Discussions*

You can generally ignore an individual Whiner. But when you happen into a nest of them at a client organization, you may find yourself on dangerous ground. If, for example, you're giving a client briefing on the status of a project and the discussion turns sour, it's your job to hear the complaints and take them back to your management team. In fact, your next step should probably be to act as catalyst to bring your team and theirs together to resolve the issues. If you discover that your client has a "we hate you, but we're putting up with you anyway because your competitors are worse" attitude, however, they may be unwilling to take the time to meet with your senior executives.

In short, they like to whine and you're caught in the middle. You're privy to some nasty comments. They disrespect you if you're disloyal to your own organization; they hate you more if you're "one of the enemy." Either way, you can't win. In such situations, it's generally best to remove yourself: "I appreciate your giving me the opportunity to sit in on these internal meetings, but I'm in a difficult position representing my organization here. I'm going to have to excuse myself from this discussion. I do hope you understand the difficulty of my situation here."

Then leave and ask not to be included in future such meetings.

THE RELATER

Relaters build long-lasting relationships with their suppliers. So how can Relaters ever be a problem? When they have relationships with incumbents and refuse even to take a look at your product or service as the new supplier wanting their business. Relaters gain security from their relationships and often let these relationships cloud their business judgment.

TIP 379: *Ask for a Level Playing Field*

State that you know they have a long-standing relationship with the current supplier, but appeal to their sense of fairness. Ask for their commitment to look at the two proposals (yours and the incumbent's) objectively.

TIP 380: *Present Your Offer in Terms of Expanded Relationships*

If relationships are important to your buyer, present your organization in terms of your network of strategic partnerships and key clients and users. For example, if you sell software, talk about your user groups and regular meetings. If you host technical experts in various exchange formats at trade associations, mention that. Show them your client list and emphasize other networking opportunities in noncompeting environments.

Subtly demonstrate to Relaters that you're asking them to trade one incumbent relationship in exchange for an entire network.

TIP 381: *Socialize First; Do Business Later*

Give Relaters a chance to get to know you first in a low-key way through industry meetings, charity events, and lunches arranged by mutual contacts. After a few casual contacts, ask for the privilege to talk business.

TIP 382: *Offer to Do the Dirty Work*

As part of your initial discussions, explain how you handle painlessly any "switch over" from an incumbent. Often a major hesitation for a Relater is the dread of breaking the news to an incumbent who has become a friend. Letting Relaters know that you handle the notification and paperwork behind the scenes eases the pain somewhat.

TIP 383: *Put the Justification in Writing*

Relaters will rethink the decision a thousand times when they envision disappointing the incumbent. You'll need to help them remember objectively why they're making the switch. Even if you don't typically do so, put your proposal in writing, listing the key benefits and a comparative analysis so they can remind themselves why the switch has become necessary and is best for their organization.

THE ROVER

Rovers show little or no loyalty to suppliers. They switch suppliers as easily and often as some people change their clothes. Rovers become disloyal customers for any number of reasons: They have a short memory about mountains you've climbed and miracles you've performed to meet their needs above and beyond normal expectations of suppliers. They always buy on price because price is much easier to understand than value. Switching vendors frequently is their method of negotiation. They like to be pursued and hate to be taken for granted.

TIP 384: *Keep Reminding Clients Why They Buy from You*

Never assume that clients realize and keep their own data on results you achieve and how your product stacks up against the competition. Send them industry articles that mention your product in a favorable light. Let them know what your test results indicate, and help them collect their own data internally to prove your value.

TIP 385: *Assume Buyers May Cancel at Any Moment*

Never give the competition a chance to "surprise" Rovers with benefits you've been providing all along—or could have been providing, had they known of these capabilities and asked.

Some clients buy out of habit year after year and, after a few years, they've forgotten why you are better than the competition. So when the competition knocks on their door, they listen. They become intrigued. They wander.

TIP 386: *Keep the Romance Alive*

Remember the thrill of the first call, the first "yes," the first appointment, the first order? How did you show your love? Let me count the ways: a lunch date; tickets to a sporting event; a call from your CEO; thank-you calls after every order—no matter how small; the "how-is-everything-going" calls during implementation; status reports on projects; the follow-up action plans after project reviews; an all-expenses-paid training session for their key managers.

When clients feel the romance fade in your relationship, they assume you don't love them anymore. A few sign on "until death do us part." Many get a wandering eye.

7

SELLING TO SENIOR EXECUTIVES

Selling to senior executives can re-
duce the sales cycle dramatically. Executives have the power to say yes,
carry the biggest checkbook, and can summon all involved parties to the
table faster. Yet survey after survey reveals the typical sales professional
does not routinely target that level. Why? Often, it's because of a lack of
access, lack of skills to sell and communicate at that level, and discomfort in relating. The guidelines in this chapter will help you to cut a
quicker path to success in the executive suite.

TIP 387: *Call at the Top, Armed with Data from
the Bottom*

Conventional wisdom says you should call as high in the organization as you can. That's good advice—if you've been able to collect all the
appropriate data beforehand to make that discussion meaningful and
relevant to the executive. Many such meetings happen, however, pre-

maturely. Sometimes it pays to call lower in the organization for your education. Talk to the line managers several layers down to find out what's not going well: What are customers complaining about? What deadlines are they missing? Where are the bottlenecks? What costs have skyrocketed, or are about to shoot up next year? Who in the organization is unhappy with your competitor and why?

Once you're armed with the data, you then have meaningful data to share with senior executives that can grab their attention.

TIP 388: *Call at the Top So That You Can Be "Delegated Down" with Authority*

Even if you create interest at the top, the reality is that frequently the senior executive will ask you to work with someone lower on the food chain either to determine whether what you offer will have significant value for the organization or to implement your recommendations. That's okay—as long as you know how to keep your foot in the executive's door.

Executive: "We may have some interest in X. That's really in Ms. Tannebaum's area of responsibility. Let me introduce you to her and you two can talk in more detail to see if we might have reason to work together."

Your response: "Thank you for that offer. I'd be happy to meet with Ms. Tannebaum. Does she have total sign-off responsibility for these kinds of projects? I was under the impression that projects of this magnitude might cross several divisions and budgets. That's why I was hoping to talk with you first—to get your input about the overall impact across several regions.

"After she and I have some exploratory discussions, I'd like to check back with you and report our findings and recommendations about how this might affect other areas. Say, in about a month?"

Wait for an affirmative nod or comment. Now when you call back for a second appointment, you already have commitment for a meeting.

Such a response lets the executive know you plan to follow protocol and work within the system to be efficient, but that you also plan to be a personal coach to keep the solution to the executive's problem or improvement to the situation on track.

TIP 389: *Understand Why Executive Decision Makers May Abdicate Authority to Underlings Who Reverse Their "Druthers"*

Even leaders of the free-world countries feel the need to consult with their advisors and gain consensus rather than simply to issue decrees. Executives do the same. Sales professionals who call on executives and expect them to give final approval on a purchase set themselves up for major disappointments on most occasions.

Instead, that executive may agree with your recommendation, give tentative approval, and then dump the decision down to the next level for final investigation and sign-off. Those who think the purchase is a "done deal" and play "one-up" with the new contact can be in for an unpleasant surprise.

Consider why executives may let underlings reverse their decisions. For example, lower-level managers may have more expertise on the subject and the executive respects that expertise. Lower-level managers also may be looking for a way to make a name for themselves, and reversing a decision to "keep the organization from making a grave mistake" may be their way of winning notoriety. In addition, they may threaten to resign if the executive buys from you. For the executive, it becomes less of a hassle to turn you down than to replace the opposing manager.

Understanding these reasons—and your odds for success if you have the wrong attitude—puts you in a better frame of mind to work with the person you're delegated down to in making things happen.

TIP 390: *Never Call on Senior Executives without Bringing Value to the Conversation*

Decide why the executive should spend valuable time with you. This may not be as difficult as you think. Many salespeople feel intimidated about calling on senior executives, because they imagine the executive paycheck equates to brilliance in areas of business and the industry specifically.

Not so. By default, these economic buyers must be generalists. They must keep their eyes on the big picture and keep many plates spinning. They rarely know what's happening on the loading dock of their own company, in the IS department during a major platform conversion, or in the customer service department—unless at least 10 percent of the client base writes a complaint to their personal attention. Frequently, industry news that floats below the level of legislation falls off their radar screens.

If you have major surveys, statistics, news about new technological advances, research on market share, or customer feedback for the future, by all means, that's valuable to executives who must devote far too much time to socializing with VIP clients and far too little time reading.

TIP 391: *Conduct Extensive Research on the Qualified Few*

Many organizations now publish biographies of senior executives on their Web site. Take your research a little further by interviewing lower-level employees and assistants for "day in the life of" vignettes, which provide insight into personalities and hobbies, quirks, values, and pet peeves.

What will you do with such information? First, you'll make sure you don't commit one of the irritants during your brief encounter. A more valuable use of the research, however, will be to discover mutual interests and to identify ways you can be of service—such as people or resources you can bring together for mutual benefit or community or charitable opportunities where you might both enjoy volunteering your time and expertise.

TIP 392: *Gain Access with Ideas You Can Deliver in a Short Appointment*

Don't be mysterious; executives don't have time for guessing games—will or won't a meeting be worthwhile? Give them enough of the idea that they'll want to hear more. If they are intrigued, they'll invite you in to discuss the details because it will reduce their investigation phase.

Examples of ideas that will open doors:

- New product ideas (borrowed from another industry or feedback from market research)
- New channel of distribution to their customers that you can help them reach through your own suppliers, partners, or other clients
- Testing that you can help do to improve a process
- Qualitative comparison data of the executive's organization to others in the industry
- Case studies of successes completed in similar organizations, with documented evidence, and ideas of how the same approach could work in the executive's organization
- Industry study about the documented cost of certain challenges the executive's organization may be having
- Industry study about the documented revenue-producing potential of a new business model
- New theory or model just published by a prestigious author, which you've applied to the executive's business, using your solutions as well to achieve maximum results

TIP 393: *Gain Access by Offering to Link Them to Someone Else*

These have always been effective door openers when a sales professional wanted an appointment to sell something to our training company. For example, Mike, a business acquaintance, called to say he'd just sold his own business and heard I might be looking for a buyer for my company (this was 12 years ago). He might be able to offer a few ideas that he'd learned in the process of selling his business and possibly link me to the same organization who bought his company.

I ask you—did I meet with him? You bet, and in the course of our later meeting, I discovered that he was currently in a new business—selling employee assessments.

Do you know of someone the executive might be interested in meeting or doing business with? Consider your own strategic partners, your other clients, or a key supplier they need. Could you help link them to a source of more qualified executives they might want to recruit? Do you have an inside track to a community of industry leaders who might be valuable resources to them as a forum for idea exchanges?

Do you have connections with the media so that they or their organization and its product or service lines could possibly be spotlighted in upcoming features or stories? Do you know a think-tank group looking for an organization to do testing on a new product that your executive's company might benefit from for little or no cost?

TIP 394: *Gain Access by Sending a Troubling Article Accompanied by a Vision or Promise of Solution*

When you run across an article in the business or industry press about a current challenge or a promising idea for future growth, clip it and send it to the executive with a cover letter saying that you'd like to have an opportunity to discuss this idea in more depth. Mention that your organization "has a solution," wants to "partner with forward-thinking companies to position for future growth to take advantage of this trend," or can provide "data on success with this approach" from other client organizations.

Leave the ball in your court. Tell the executive when you'll call to follow up and verify interest in setting up a meeting.

TIP 395: *Gain Access by Becoming a Shareholder*

Buy a few shares in a prospect's company. Attend the annual shareholders meeting. Meet the executive during the meeting—as a shareholder, not a salesperson.

TIP 396: *Gain Access by Becoming a Recognized Expert in the Industry*

If you've been marketing yourself in the industry, you have been submitting proposals to speak at industry meetings, accepting invitations to participate on panels, writing articles in trade journals, making yourself available for interviews with the business press, and writing letters to the editor of newspapers and the business and industry publications. You may serve as an officer in your trade association or on a key task force to solve an industry problem or meeting before Congress about pending legislation.

Once you're recognized as an industry leader, executives often see you as a peer who can "consult" with them and provide valuable insights. They will think twice before creating a negative impression by declining an invitation to meet with you, because they understand that your network spans the breadth of the industry leadership.

TIP 397: *Gain Access during Their Transition Period*

Look for executives new on the job. They need a quick start and are looking for people with insights about new approaches and with experience from other industries that might translate to theirs. They have fewer people calling on them and haven't yet decided who has the most credibility among their suppliers. The door cracks open slightly wider during this phase.

TIP 398: *Gain Access during Transition of Your Contact*

When the lower-level employee leaves, take that as an opportunity to extend your reach to the next rung on the ladder. Before your contact says goodbye, don't ask to be introduced to the incoming person; ask to be introduced to the boss. If your contact refuses, just bide your time until they walk out the door. You can then start fresh on the executive floor.

TIP 399: *Gain Access When You Have Media Exposure for Them*

To discover how to take advantage of marketing opportunities with the media, refer to Chapter 8. Seek out opportunities to contact senior executives to interview them, quote them, or highlight their organization.

Above all, make response easy, but don't make it routine. That is, don't make your questions something they'll forward to the PR department to handle for them. Pose only two or three questions that they must answer personally—something that their PR person couldn't respond to without interviewing them first.

Give the executive time to think before responding. Unless your topic is time sensitive, the typical protocol is to send a letter or e-mail requesting the interview. Explain that you're doing a "round-up" article for X industry or business journal, and that you've selected three executives to interview and would like to see if Ms. VIP would be willing to spend about 8 to 12 minutes with you to answer the enclosed questions. Then list the questions. The administrative assistant will most likely call back to schedule the phone interview or appointment.

One caveat: Make sure the topic of your article and the questions you ask merit the executive's time and pique his or her interest.

TIP 400: *Gain Access by Exposure in the Publications They Read*

Write letters to the editor, brief articles, or Op Ed (opinion editorial) pieces on industry or social issues that affect executives. Be sure to include your name and contact information. Some publications drop off the contact information, but executives have smart assistants who can find you. (For more details, see Chapter 8 on marketing.)

TIP 401: *Gain Access by Playing Where They Play—In Your Own Backyard*

Where do the executives play golf, racquetball, tennis, or jog? Where do they dine out? Where do they work out? Where do they travel on vacation?

This used to be an easy question, but not anymore. For example, for years travelers justified first-class airfare by insisting they'd meet other executives in the seat beside them and maybe gain a prospect. 'Taint so today. First class now is filled with frequent fliers—road warriors who may be technicians traveling from Nome, Alaska, to Jacksonville, Florida, weekly to troubleshoot software systems; consultants working on engineering plans for a city's roadways; or tax accountants reviewing a client's records. After 9/11 when so many found themselves grounded at inconvenient spots around the globe, executives have managed to stay closer to home.

Research by authors of books such as *The Millionaire Next Door* and *The Millionaire Mind,* as well as of articles in magazines such as *Fast Company,* report a big distinction between the truly wealthy and the high-income individual. The truly wealthy build assets that provide them true freedom for the long haul; the high-income earners, on the other hand, tend to earn a lot and spend more. While high-income earners often collect possessions, take exotic vacations, and play hard with all the typical status symbols, the truly wealthy often spend their leisure time on the simple things—time with family and friends, entertainment at home.

According to author Thomas Stanley, one of the top authorities on America's truly wealthy, they do not buy tickets to opening nights at the theatre, routinely take exotic weekends away, hire chauffeurs or gardeners or cooks, or have tennis courts in the backyard.

The bottom line: Playing where executives play doesn't always mean extra expense. You don't necessarily have to stretch beyond your limits. The most successful executives may play near home and dine out at McDonald's with their grandchildren quite often.

Yes, of course, chances are greater that hour per hour you'll meet more executives at the country club than you will at Burger King. But you can increase your odds dramatically by simply asking a few questions of those in the know and being alert to *individual lifestyles.*

TIP 402: *Gain Access by Serving Where They Serve*

Senior executives typically contribute a good amount of time to community and charitable activities such as fundraisers, program committees, nonprofit boards, or membership drives. Find such places of services and go to work. You'll likely get to know your prospects and build a personal relationship with them that will lead them to ask: "So what do you do?" "Who are some of your clients?" "Why don't you come out and talk to us sometime?"

TIP 403: *Gain Access with a Title Match*

Approach one of the executives in your own organization, share all your research on the account you want to crack, and ask if they'd be willing to join you in a meeting with the executive in the prospective organization.

Top executives pay attention to rank. Many CEOs have each other on their mailing lists—they share their annual stockholder reports, news releases, and congratulatory notes for company and personal achievements. The CEO circle stays small. When another executive joins the meeting, the request receives much more serious attention than that simply from Joe or Joanna Smoe, general sales professional.

Find someone with a close title match in your own organization to the executive you want to see in the prospect's organization, and set about to link them up so you can ride the coattails.

TIP 404: *Profile an Executive's Personality Before You Plan Your Approach*

Executive personalities reflect the rest of humanity: You have drivers, analyticals, socializers, and so forth to match almost any personality test on the market. One of my CEO friends, Ken, has a president to run his company and spends most of his time on a yacht, entertaining clients. That lifestyle would bore other executives half to death.

Another CEO acquaintance prefers to be at his desk by 6:00 every morning and puts in at least 12 hours a day—almost without pausing for people or meals.

Needless to say, selling to them—or even meeting with them—requires a different tactic. This is where befriending assistants and talking with mutual acquaintances in the industry or organization can give you guidance.

TIP 405: *Respect the Executive-Assistant System*

Midlevel managers sometimes "inherit" their assistants. This is not so with most executives. Either they have hand-selected their assistants or have acquired those already on the job and determined them to be an efficient, capable member of the team. These people serve a vital role in maintaining the executive's efficiency, so the executive expects you to work within the system they've created for effective time and project management.

Never consider the assistants to a top executive as gatekeepers to be challenged, lied to, or thwarted. Treat them with the same respect you would show the executive. Consider them a team.

TIP 406: *Write First If You Have No Connection*

For the outsider, protocol with senior executives among themselves is to write first rather than call for an appointment. For the most part, they write to say they'll be calling when they're in town to have lunch. They write each other to say: "Congratulations on this year's company performance—I just read your annual report and things look promising." "I saw in *The Wall Street Journal* last week that the lawsuit was settled out of court. I know that settlement lifted a burden off your shoulders. Will be looking to see your stock prices soar."

When you catch the executive or their administrative assistant on the phone and state your case, the answer is almost always no or it depends. They don't know enough to say yes.

But a letter changes things. When considering an appointment with an outsider, if the executive has something in writing about whom you are, what you want, and how much time you will need, it makes it much easier to juggle priorities on the calendar. A letter lays out the case. It gives legitimacy to the request, and it allows the assistant to research you and your organization and fit you into the priorities of the week or month.

Granted, it may delay your getting in to see the executive, but when you arrive, you will have the executive's focus—until you lose it yourself.

TIP 407: *State the Purpose of the Meeting and How Long It Will Take*

Senior executives do not respond well to vague agendas such as: "I'd like to explore possible ways we might work together to save you some money." "The purpose of the meeting would be to introduce you to our services." "I'd like to discuss some industry trends that you might find surprising and that might help you prepare for the future." Every other person on the planet wanting to see that executive could state virtually that same purpose. Your agenda must be more targeted and intriguing.

Also state a time limit—20 minutes, half an hour—so that the executives know what time investment they are risking. Be sure to stay within that allotted time unless the executives themselves *clearly* extend it.

TIP 408: *Gain Interest Fast*

Plan your opening comment. Don't assume that something appropriately witty or interesting will "hit you" when you walk in the door. Check the company's stock price; if it's going up, offer congratulations. (If it's going down, ask why. You may want to do this a little later in the discussion, however, rather than open on a negative note.) If the CEO has just hired a new executive on the team, mention that. If they've just introduced a new product into the market, ask or comment on how well it's doing. Have they just signed a new strategic partnership agreement? Congratulate them and ask or comment about what avenues that opens for them.

You also could mention something from the "What's News?" column from the *Wall Street Journal.* You can be sure every executive has read it that day. If they've missed it for some reason, they'll be eager to know what hot story they missed and you can fill them in quickly before you move on to the topic of your business.

Never waste an executive's time on a fact-finding mission. Do your homework before you arrive so you won't have to ask a question such as: "What year was it that you merged with Universal, Inc.?" Executives become bored, then skeptical, then hostile very fast.

TIP 409: *Never Waste an Executive's Time—And Never Fail to Establish Rapport*

These two guidelines are not mutually exclusive. At the beginning of your meeting, don't make the mistake of starting out on non-business issues. Executives will become restless and suspicious; their time is at a premium and they know your primary motive is not to discuss their golf game, cruise, or gourmet cooking interests. Instead, connect on business issues first.

That said, never fail to connect with senior executives on a personal note as well. This works best at the end of your discussion, once they have come to trust that you respect their time and do not intend to use the personal connection to manipulate them.

Rapport is not just the handle on the executive door—it must play a part in an ongoing relationship. Rapport comes after you have established clear, straightforward communication and a mutual respect of expertise and time.

TIP 410: *Understand That Top Executives* Are Not *Necessarily Interested in Solutions to Current Problems*

Lower-level buyers primarily concern themselves with how a product or service works and how the cost compares to that of your competitors. Can they justify any differential to their higher-ups? Middle managers concern themselves with product or service performance in their functional areas of responsibility. What problems does the product or service solve this next month, quarter, or year?

Senior executives, on the other hand, have their radar screens scanning the next 2 to 20 years. They focus on the financial success of the total organization for the current quarter and then very long term.

They'll want answers to these questions: What are other organizations in the industry doing? Do you have a novel way to look at my business? Can you challenge my assumptions or shift my thinking to help me see issues in a new light? What new ideas do you have for me that might fundamentally change the way we do business? What business, technological, or social trends do you see that I should prepare for? What can you tell me to help me take advantage of the changes coming our way? How will this product or service improve the overall profitability of the enterprise?

TIP 411: *Serve as a Consultant*

Arrive at your first appointment with a mind-set to serve, not sell. That means you'll prepare, armed with knowledge of the prospect's industry and research on the organization. Where do you find such inside information? You can start with annual reports for publicly held companies. You'll find their goals and strategic objectives stated there, along with what's important to the CEO (emphasized in the letter to the shareholders).

From this information, you'll prepare provocative questions to guide the discussion:

- How would you prioritize your goals?
- What progress have you made so far toward your goals?
- How are you monitoring your progress toward these goals?
- Who's leading the charge for each goal?
- What obstacles have you run into so far in achieving this year's goals?
- What has contributed to your success in each area?
- What changes in the marketplace or in your own organization have led you to set these initiatives?
- How will achieving these goals position your organization for the next five years?
- How does your success in these areas affect your standing with your own customers?
- Have you picked up ideas from other industries that you've been able to translate to your own organization?
- What are others in your industry doing that you're not doing? Why not? How successful have they been in these areas?
- If you can improve one thing about last quarter's performance, what would that be?
- What's your biggest area for growth in the next five years—adding new products/services, looking for new distribution channels, or opening new markets altogether?
- What are your most important customers asking you to do now?
- What would you have to change to be able to provide that profitably?
- What's the most important thing you could do to contribute to your most important customer's success?
- What would you have to do to bring in the biggest new client you've ever signed?

As a result, by the end of the meeting, the executive should see you as a valuable peer who wants to serve—and you will be armed with answers that should help you find selling opportunities on later visits.

Your first goal, then, must be to sell yourself as a strategic partner.

TIP 412: *Position Your Solution for Second-Generation Work*

The mission of lower-level managers is to improve their own organization. Executives know that to capture future growth they will continually have to find ways to help their customers serve *their customers*—second-generation work. How will your solution improve the business of your customer's customers? Tell it to the executives and you have their attention.

TIP 413: *Overview Your Ideas in 60 Seconds or Less*

The world has become accustomed to sound bites, and so have executives. Chances are that they have had media training to deliver them. Write your message. Then edit out the garbage. If you can't write it clearly, you can't say it succinctly. If you need help, study the jacket flaps on business books for the sound bites that summarize bestsellers—that entice a buyer to pluck down $20 for one book versus another.

You have to make executives understand the idea quickly or they're on to something else. Be simple, specific, and concrete.

TIP 414: *Take Control of the First Call or Meeting*

Certainly, senior executives call the shots on most occasions; however, they are perfectly willing for you to drive if you show them you know how to get to the destination.

Have a plan. At the very beginning, either tell them or show them (brief written agenda) how you plan to spend your 20 to 30 minutes together. "I know you're busy and our time together is short, so here's what I thought would be important to cover: X, Y, and Z. Does that sound on target to you?"

Then take off. You always can alter the agenda if the executive leads in another direction, but they will be happy to know you respect their time and have a road map. In fact, you'll see their face visibly relax.

TIP 415: *Focus on Stories, Not Statistics*

Stories make your points memorable. Data are for the middle managers. Statistics and charts support your key points and give you credibility—but they do not stay in the mind. If they did, every TV commercial you hear would be announcers reading test results and survey data. Make your points about the solutions you're selling with well-chosen business stories from client organizations. Reduce the case histories to the pertinent details—sound bites that they can then convey to their advisors in later meetings when they're retelling your story.

TIP 416: *Plan on a Dialogue, Not a Monologue*

When giving a formal presentation to a group of executives, make sure your delivery and format take into account interactivity. Build your structure around key questions you think the executives will want answered, and then pause for feedback or follow-up questions. You also can focus on key objectives or goals, your solutions to achieve those goals, the results you expect, and supporting facts for each result presented. Then pause for related questions and feedback. The idea is not to plan on giving a half-hour formal presentation, nonstop, without input—no matter how well your sponsor has prepared you.

The name of the game with executives is dialogue, not monologue.

TIP 417: *Be Ready with Plan B*

Count on senior executives to ask tough questions about your recommendations—your ideal plan for what should happen if the organization buys your product or service and all goes well. How do you plan to handle obstacles that may crop up to thwart progress?

You'll need to have thought through these issues and have a contingency plan for every what-if. Otherwise, executives are likely to dismiss your ideas as pie-in-the-sky plans that need far more thought than they can afford to devote to the matter. Enter task force or committee.

TIP 418: *Leave a One-Page Synopsis*

Senior executives need to have a walk-away piece to use for when they consult with other advisors and have no time to spend explaining what you took 20 to 30 minutes to overview. You should provide a one-page, strategic overview for that purpose. Make it compelling, clear, concrete, complete, concise, and correct. Don't count on slapping something together for that purpose in an hour before you show up for the meeting.

TIP 419: *Dress to Create an Executive Image*

"Business casual" has confused far too many sales professionals. Executives may "dress down" in their own organization to give the appearance of being "one of the troops," to be comfortable, or to create a casual atmosphere. As an outsider, you have a different purpose and need to create a different image. In a word, the image you want to create is quality. Buy the highest quality clothes and accessories that you can afford.

However, quality does not always come with a matching price tag. If you know what you're looking for and are an excellent shopper, you can find it at a lower price. Shop at quality stores. Ask salesclerks what makes jacket A of higher quality than jacket B, what makes wallet C more expensive that wallet D, and what makes shoes E last longer than shoes F. Armed with that knowledge, you'll know a bargain when you find the item elsewhere with a lower price tag.

Generally, fabric (wool, silk, 100 percent cotton) and styling equate to quality clothes that wear well over time and hold their shape. If you stay with classics—versus faddish styles that come and go by season—you will be able to buy better quality clothes and always look well dressed.

Jewelry should be conservative, not flashy. Prefer to buy fewer pieces of higher quality than many pieces of trendy costume jewelry.

Hair should be cut in a conservative, flattering style to fit your face and lifestyle. If it looks as though you spent a lot of time on it (oils, mousses, gels)—or no time at all—you'll be out of place in the executive boardroom.

In general, dress, accessories, and grooming (makeup, beard, fingernails, fragrance, shoe shines) should be meticulous, elegant, conservative, and classy.

TIP 420: *Don't Ask for the Business*

Your goal is to walk in the senior executive's door as a peer—and never back up. Shifting into "sales mode" from a peer role definitely becomes a step backward. Once you've initiated a dialogue as a trusted advisor, you certainly don't want to try to pressure senior executives into a spur-of-the-moment decision, even when they have shown great interest in your idea or offering.

Instead, at the point of close, you want to let them lead to the next step. At the very most, you may want to suggest a next step with a question or comment: "So what's the next step?" "Okay, where do we go from here?" "Shall I get with Mark to work out the details about X?" "Let's set something up in about two weeks to go over the plan for X. Will that give you time to talk this over with your team? Maybe they'd like to meet with us then."

Senior executives know how to get things done. When they hear an idea they like, they will act on it. They have held their position in the boardroom by doing that very thing—taking action. Trying to push a senior executive is a self-defeating slip-up for the salesperson.

TIP 421: *Write as a Second Alternative*

Occasionally, you find top executives who are such tight time managers that they won't risk meeting with you without first seeing your value on paper. When that's the case, state your purpose or offering briefly in a letter or a one- or two-page proposal—just enough to sell the idea of talking in detail. Present the benefits as specifically as possible—what you hope to achieve either in a meeting or with your product or service.

Be sure to include proof or evidence that you can deliver, such as samples of your work or case studies of successful projects with satisfied clients. Finally, ask for the meeting or the telephone appointment.

Putting it in writing serves the same purpose as a peephole in the front door.

8

MARKETING YOURSELF AND GENERATING LEADS

I know, I know, I know: The Marketing people get paid to do the marketing and produce the leads; the salespeople sell. In theory, it's a beautiful plan, but in the reality of today's marketplace, superstar salespeople generate their own leads in addition to what the organization may send their way.

Of course, for thousands of entrepreneurs, small business owners, independents, and sales professionals from small to midsized organizations, that has been the game plan all along: You live and die, sell or don't sell, by your own ability to market and generate leads.

Some do it well; some don't. To use a computer analogy, consider marketing your source code. Tips in this chapter will help you design the code and program your selling system to spit out leads to close the sale you need to exceed your income goals.

SPEAKING

TIP 422: *Understand the Value of Speaking as a Marketing Tool*

You don't have to look far to make speaking pay off as a prospecting and marketing technique. You'll find opportunities at local civic, fraternal, and business organizations, which are always needing monthly speakers on business topics at industry and professional conferences; at trade shows; and at various symposiums sponsored by universities.

Additionally, your organization or you and a few colleagues can create and host your own educational seminars or showcases. The best thing about these events is that leads from such events prequalify themselves. Buyers attend because they're already interested in the issues being addressed.

Other platforms for speaking include VIP appreciation/recognition events, chamber of commerce events, and charities and foundation events and meetings.

Speaking involves work, yes, but the payoff can be tremendous. Such events have legs—that is, you can accomplish several goals at once:

- You can invite prospects to attend and give them something of value with important content.
- You can generate spin-off leads and referrals.
- You can increase visibility within your own organization to generate referrals from colleagues as you notify them about the upcoming event. (They may not have anyone to send, but they'll remember that you're doing the event and associate you with your expertise for the subject.)
- You also can take the opportunity to service your long-term clients—invite those who've already purchased from you just as a "value-added" benefit.

You'll be disappointed, however, if you expect to close sales at such speaking events. Your goal should be to network with as many people as possible and gather names for later, individual follow-up to talk in depth. If you spend time talking in depth to any single individual, you'll miss the broader goal of connecting with many.

Your goal is to walk away with business cards from those attendees who've said: "Why don't you call me."

TIP 423: *Get Your Expertise Documented by Others in the Industry by Your Invitations to Speak*

The value of PR from speaking spreads much wider than those in attendance. Each year for the past 22 years, I've spoken at the international conference for my professional association. Through the years, the attendance has grown from about 4,000 to well over 14,000 annually. The marketing reach, however, goes well beyond that.

For starters, the association does several pre- and postconference mailings to its total membership of approximately 70,000 buyers. In addition, there are listings in the program bulletins each day of the conference; conference audio recordings, complete with the names and companies of presenters; preconvention articles submitted by the presenters included in e-newsletters sent to the membership to generate interest for the convention; and presenters' bios and organizations listed on the Web site for several months before the conference.

Much of this publicity goes to those who don't even show up for your event! The message they receive is: "This industry recognizes this individual or organization as a leader in the industry." *You're* not saying you know what you're talking about—the industry spokespeople have documented that fact in their brochures.

TIP 424: *Ask a Hot Prospect or Key Client to Join You on an Opinion Panel*

Identify an emerging trend or a challenging or a controversial issue that organizations in your industry must grapple with, and then ask a hot prospect or a prestigious client if they would be willing to join you on the platform at an upcoming meeting or trade show to address the issue. In fact, you might decide to moderate a panel and invite two or three such guests to express their opinions on the issues. Or, you might share the work or research you and your organization have done on the issue and then use a client organization as the case study. Ask your client to elaborate on how this situation has affected their organization or how the organization has met the challenge successfully.

You do all the work and get all the leads from the session, and your client or prospect shares in the PR spotlight.

TIP 425: *Plan Ways to Mention Your Product, Service, or Organization Subtly Rather Than Blatantly*

Your audience will protest loudly if your speech becomes a sales pitch. You can't use the speaking opportunity simply to tell about what your company offers and go directly through a list of benefits. But, of course, conference attendees at industry meetings know that you don't spend $2,000 and two days' time to fly across country just to help them build a better a mousetrap unless you get some cheese for yourself.

The key to giving your buyer audience a beneficial, educational session while still letting those who might be interested know what you do so they can follow up with you is to plan *how* to make mention of your product or service and *when* to do so. Here are three ideas in that regard:

1. Choose anecdotes to illustrate key points that showcase your expertise.

2. Put descriptive slogans on your handouts and any other reference materials.

3. Have an introducer mention your organization and establish credibility.

The other key ingredient in buyer acceptance is when to plug your organization or product or service: Give value first, provide contact information later. Interested buyers will follow up or ask you to follow up. It rarely works the other way.

TIP 426: *Invite Group Participation or Questions to Establish Individual Links*

Make your presentation a conversation with a group of 200 rather than between two. Aim to create a dialogue rather than a performance. Invite your buyers to share their concerns about your topic; ask questions from the floor; or stand up in groups of four and take two minutes to express to each other their biggest problem with X, or relate frustrating experiences they've had with Y, and challenges they're hoping to solve in the next 12 months. (Challenges, of course, your product or service can help address!)

TIP 427: *Provide Multiple Avenues to Your Front Door*

Sponsors of most conferences take great care to make sure that speakers don't turn their sessions into sales pitches. Speakers who do rarely get invited back a second time. Even if that weren't the case—unless you have colleagues and assistants traveling with you—as one person, you don't have time to talk with all the people waiting to shake your hand and ask you detailed questions after you speak. Some are interested buyers; some are not. But you never know which are which at the moment and they all take time in the after-session shuffle.

Consider several ways to make it easy for those who want to contact you later. You can put your contact information at the bottom of any slides used during your presentation, on brochures or walk-away pieces, or on invitations for follow-up events. You can give them a reason to go to your Web site—for example, to download handouts, for a copy of your slides, for a list of ten tips on X, or for a bibliography on Y.

TIP 428: *Arrive Early and Stay Late*

A good educational session involves more than valuable information. To advance your prospecting methods, you need to establish personal connection—not be just another "session" or meeting someone attended. That means taking the time to mingle with the group to find out what organizations are represented, what their needs are, why they're in your session, how they plan to use your information, or if they're the buyer or only the collector of information. These will be your follow-up contacts afterward.

The people who chitchat with you will be your grassroots supporters, referring you to their colleagues who need your products and services even when they themselves can't buy.

TIP 429: *Be Stingy with Your Business Cards*

Ask interested prospects for their business card rather than providing yours. When you hand prospects your cards, you're dependent on them to follow up. When you get their cards, you can retain control and take the next step. Of course, you can always *exchange* cards." The only problem with putting your card in their hands is this response when you call: "I have your contact information. When there's a need, I'll be in touch." You, however, want the opportunity to *create* the need.

TIP 430: *Never "Go It Alone"*

Why do grocery stores put gum, candy, magazines, and batteries in the racks near the cashier checkout stands? Why do movie theatres locate the concession stands near the entrances to the seating?

We're an impatient culture. Buyers balk at waiting. If you have a long line of well-wishers and questioners surrounding you after your session, that may be great for the ego—but bad for prospecting. Prospects make impulsive contact with you—or not, depending on your availability. Take a buddy, an assistant, or several others to field questions. You should plan a specific time in the session to let the group know who's part of your organization so impatient attendees can approach them if you're unavailable while talking with other people.

WRITING—DIRECT MAIL, E-MAIL, NEWSLETTERS, AND WEB PAGES

TIP 431: *Understand the Value of Writing as a Marketing Tool*

Writing represents a good prospecting tool that few salespeople take advantage of—either because they think they don't have the skills or because they think it takes a long time. Often, a letter or an e-mail to an editor can be written in the same amount of time it takes to make a few prospecting calls and the "Letters (or E-mail) to the Editor" section is the most widely read section of most publications.

If fear that you don't have the skill is holding you back, think again. We're not talking about penning the great American novel or movie script. We're talking about a business letter or article. If you can speak clearly, concisely, and coherently, you can write well enough to publish a short e-mail, letter, or article.

This skill and a few minutes can ensure that you, your product, service, or organization takes center stage before thousands of prospects.

TIP 432: *Write E-mails or Letters to the Editor for Publication in Trade Journals and the Business Press*

Do you see an industry trend that you can wax eloquently about? Have you read a recent journal article with which you strongly agree or disagree? Put your opinions in writing, and sign your name, product/service, and company.

Instead of simply reacting to something you've read in the journal or business paper, raise a new issue, express your opinion, or pose a provocative question for other readers to jump into the fray. Again, be sure to sign your name, product or service, and company. Example: Joe Smoe, Sales Rep for XYZ Products, ABC Company.

As you comment on important industry issues, you'll position yourself as an expert. Editors will add you to their database for later articles and quotes.

Prospects will find you. They'll e-mail the magazine or call your company and ask for you—either to argue with you or talk with you because "you certainly know what you're talking about" and they'll want to deal with a knowledgeable, witty person like you.

TIP 433: *Get Your Expertise Documented by Industry Leaders by Being Interviewed and Quoted in Articles*

To get quoted—hopefully, with a mention of your product or service and your organization—write a "not for publication" letter or e-mail to the editor of an industry publication and offer hot story ideas before other editors or reporters think of them. Be sure to tie your "news" to a big trend, issue, or problem, and be prepared to suggest other names as interviewees. Rarely do reporters do a story with only one source. (Yes, unfortunately, you'll have to provide competitors' names, but what key editor of a trade journal wouldn't already know your competitors? Besides, if you're the one providing the most help, you'll most likely get the most ink.)

Do your homework before the interview and jot down some key phrases, analogies, or anecdotes. Be ready to provide survey results, statistics, or other hard data, if possible. That kind of information almost always makes it into an article—and gets linked to your organization and your name specifically as the source. Be colorful and controversial. But never ask to review the article before publication. That's a big no-no. Reporters and editors take that as an insult.

TIP 434: *Write an Article to Be Published in the Business or Industry Trade Journal*

Don't wait for an invitation, however, from some editor to recognize your expertise and interview you or ask you to submit an article. (By the way, not only will authorship bring you prospects, but it will bring you recognition within your own organization. Several companies offer their employees nice bonuses for getting articles placed in business or trade publications because they understand the value of editorial content versus paid-for advertising.)

The following guidelines will help you create articles that get attention from busy prospects:

- Use a "hook" to answer why the topic is important today. Make sure the information is timely.
- Add sidebars of helpful checklists. Example: "How do you know if your organization needs a tune-up?"
- Use pullouts of provocative points, intriguing comments, or revealing statistics. The more controversial the better.

- Add headings to grab skimming readers. Make them either informative or intriguing.
- Include your bio, with full contact information. Be brief but always include your organization and product line. Editors may delete specific product names, but sometimes they get by. Interested prospects will call to inquire—if you've been helpful to them. You'll double your response rate if you tell them to call for a handy tip sheet or a reference guide of further information.
- Leave wide margins, add full headers, and omit staples—logistics count with harried editors.

TIP 435: *Invite a Client to Coauthor a "Case History" Article with You*

Double your money and reward by asking an important client to join you in the limelight. You do all the work—write the article—and let your client have the recognition. That is, query the editor for the go-ahead on the article idea and then basically outline your key points.

With a key client, the majority of the details of the article will focus on the client's organization. You'll be making your client contact and other employees of the organization the heroes in the story.

Writing a case history article will have several benefits:

- It will strengthen your client relationship.
- It will impress the individual buyer at your client's organization—that you have access to the press. They will "owe you one" for making them a star in the media before their own people.

Other prospective clients in similar situations will read of your results with that organization and wonder if you can achieve the same results for them.

Editors will view you as an expert for other stories and quotes.

TIP 436: *Invite Prospects to Contribute a "Round-Up" Article*

With a targeted prospect, your article will take a different approach, but have essentially the same benefits as a case history article with a client. You will outline key points about a trend, issue, or problem in the industry, and then call several people to ask their opinions and how they are facing the challenge. In doing so, you're positioning yourself with these prospects as an industry leader, a problem solver, a peer advisor, and a catalyst to make things happen for the future.

TIP 437: *Use Your Reprints to Gain Their Full Value*

Getting articles published represents only the tip of the proverbial iceberg of this marketing effort. Have your article reprinted and send it to your list of prospects. Simply attach your card with a brief note saying: "Thought you might be interested if you're experiencing some of these same issues in your organization." No need to point out that you wrote the article—the prospect will see your photo and bio on the article.

You also can have your sales manager send out the article under their signature. A more formal cover letter (that you might draft yourself to get it done faster) might imply that the article was being sent to the database of the entire organization—raising your stock in the eye of the lonely buyer you call on quarter after quarter.

The value in writing is rarely in writing—but in having written. Reprint. Reprint. Reprint.

TIP 438: *Write a White Paper for Internal or External Publication*

A white paper takes a position; it expresses an opinion—usually a strong opinion—on an issue where everyone seems to be either in a state of confusion or in total disagreement.

The white paper can be an attempt to say: "Here's the research and explanation that will clear up all the confusion." It also can be an attempt to grab attention and create more controversy for a startling new perspective.

Published internally for your own organization, a white paper can set you apart as the guru for your product line. It might present "feedback from the field"—challenges from customers and new features they have been asking for in new designs for future product releases. A white paper might explain how important on-time delivery and customer service is to ongoing sales.

In an externally published white paper, you will not mention your product or organization directly. Your goal will be to provide useful information to the industry and position yourself as an expert on a topic. Indirectly, of course, you will become the go-to person and organization when readers get ready to buy.

TIP 439: *Create and Distribute a Newsletter Online, by Direct Mail, or Packaged with Your Product or Service*

Entire books have been written on the value of newsletters to stay in touch with clients and prospects, as well as newsletters to generate revenue. We're not talking about your taking time to create an eight-page, full-color, graphic-enhanced monthly newsletter. (Although, once an electronic masthead is set up, that kind of newsletter is not all that time-consuming.)

But many salespeople have discovered that even a one- to two-page newsletter containing valuable tips on topics of interest keeps their name in front of clients and prospects and brings in new leads regularly.

Ours probably breaks the record for brevity. Our *Communication Tip of the Month* contains only one communication tip—typically about 6 to 20 lines long—from our various training programs (business or technical writing, sales presentations, proposal development, interpersonal skills, sales, customer service, grammar, or personal productivity). It goes out once a month to keep our name in front of prospects and clients—and only to those who sign up from our Web site at <www.booher.com>, from workshop attendance, or by requests during prospecting calls.

Our four-page newsletter, *The Confident Communicator,* goes out once a quarter. Neither takes enormous effort, but both generate leads while providing clients and prospects with valuable information.

TIP 440: *Create "Fact Sheets" or Reference Information*

Think about the questions clients typically ask you during the product or service implementation phase. What additional information could you provide clients and prospects that they would consider useful and would be easy for you to develop?

For example, financial institutions provide charts to show how pretax returns compare to tax-exempt investments at the various income-bracket levels. Businesses in the hotel industry occasionally give out guides on customary tipping for various services in foreign countries. A rep for a manufacturer product line gives out a chart that converts the metric units to their English-unit equivalents.

Post such information online on your personal Website. Offer it as a giveaway at the end of published articles. Package it with your product or service when you mail it. E-mail it to prospects in response to inquiries from ads, quizzes, or assessments.

TIP 441: *Create Opt-In E-mail Reminders to Buy— Special Offers, New Products or Services, Special Recognitions*

E-mail marketing has experienced many changes during the past few years. In the beginning, e-mail marketing gurus hyped it as the ultimate marketing tool—fast, inexpensive, and measurable. Marketers counted click-through rates to tout their success because people, by and large, opened and read just about everything that landed in their in-box.

Today, the talk is about spam and how it can kill your image. According to a recent DoubleClick study, 78 percent of American e-mail users surveyed said they *wanted to receive e-mail* from their favorite online suppliers. According to a study recently released by The Association of Interactive Marketing and The Direct Marketing Association, 63 percent of the companies surveyed reported that e-mail marketing was their most effective customer-retention effort.

Their secret? Permission-based e-mail.

Consider making a special effort to get the e-mail addresses of both customers and prospects. Here are four ideas to do that:

1. Ask for their e-mail address, explaining that you like to send announcements on new products and services and special offers from time to time. If they give it to you with that explanation, you can assume their permission.

2. Offer a sign-up option on your personal Web site (see Tip 442).

3. Offer other freebies, such as a newsletter, reference guide, or tip sheet, that require your customers and prospects to provide their e-mail address. Then send the first e-mail promotion, providing clear instructions on how to unsubscribe to future e-mail announcements or updates from you.

4. Use your voicemail greeting to collect e-mail addresses. Example: "This is Joe Smoe. I will be in client meetings all day today, May 6, but will be picking up messages every few hours. You can leave a

message on my cell at 972-555-3344 or e-mail me at joe.smoe@UT .com. Or, if you'll leave me YOUR e-mail, it may be faster to get in touch that way."

What separates the effective from the ineffective email reminders? According to Internet marketing guru Corey Rudl <www.marketingtips .com>, you should pay attention to several things to ensure success. First, make sure that what you send is directly relevant to your buyers' interests. If they opted in to hear more about financial planning, don't send them an e-mail about costume jewelry you make and sell as a hobby. Second, proofread everything you send. Third, verify that you don't have format glitches by signing up for a free e-mail address on all the most popular services like Hotmail, Yahoo!, and Juno, and then test how your e-mail looks when it lands in your buyers' boxes.

So what do you send? You'll definitely want to leave the general marketing promotions to your organization's marketing staff. You should, however, send your own brief e-mail reminders, but be sure to keep them warm and personal. Here are a few reasons you can use to get in touch:

- Offer a tip sheet, special report, or article of valuable information on a timely subject
- Announce a new product or service
- Tell clients about special discounts or promotions
- Inform clients about a special recognition won by your organization that builds credibility for your products or services, and then focus on the benefits/results
- Showcase a client "hero" for their success with one of your products

TIP 442: *Create a Personal Web Site to Generate Leads*

Direct prospects to your own Web site to download such helpful information as the items mentioned in previous tips. On your site, archive your own past published articles and ask for referrals and details of your clients' case histories on your products and services. To let your clients see you in a more personal light—not just as a "business contact"—post a photo or two of yourself and your family enjoying a hobby or family outing. For example, my financial broker, representing one of the largest and most conservative firms in the country and advising clients on investments involving millions of dollars, sent out a postcard of her family enjoying a barbecue in the backyard. Another colleague posted photos of his biking trip through the Swiss Alps. Such a site can go a long way in building a personal relationship with good clients.

TIP 443: *Use a Combination of Direct Mail and Phone Calls to Generate the Most Attention*

Despite e-mail, direct mail still has its place in prospecting: It creates credibility before you call; it gives you a "reason" to call; and it's expected protocol with senior executives. In addition, repetition increases name recognition for calls—it takes less time than follow-up calls to low-priority prospects, and it keeps your name in front of prospects during "lulls."

If the prospect hasn't read your letter or e-mail before you call, don't worry. You can refer to it anyway and summarize what it said. The fact that you sent it creates an impression and establishes legitimacy.

However, there's no research to prove that people pay more attention to direct mail than to phone calls or e-mail. Some people delete all e-mail unless they recognize the sender. Because almost all business people have access to e-mail, first-class mail has dwindled dramatically. This makes personal letters stand out—and increases the likelihood they'll be read. On the other hand, to some people phone calls seem more urgent and gets their immediate attention best.

The bottom line: You can argue a good case for both strategies, depending on what you're offering and who your prospects are. Try both strategies, and keep records to determine which works best for you.

TIP 444: *Compose a Business Message, Not a "Sales" Letter*

Don't make your letter look as though the Marketing Department prepared it and sent it to everyone on a purchased list. If you're sending an e-mail, make sure it doesn't look like something coming from a listserv.

First-class letters are rare these days. They get attention. Compose a business message—yes, a sales *pull,* but not a sales *look.*

Want an example? Take the pile of mail coming to your home any day of the week. Stand four feet away from it and have someone else open it for you. Ask them to hold each piece toward you so that you can glance at it from a distance. Can't you tell without reading them which are sales letters to be tossed in the trash and which are important messages that you need to read—for example, from your lawyer, accountant, or doctor?

So can your prospects. Avoid sending the letter that looks like a mass mailing from a marketing team: two-color ink, maybe a photo or two, several different font sizes, a generic opening, vague phrasing throughout.

Send your prospects messages that sound like a personal communication—not hype that will be tossed away.

TIP 445: *Create an Appealing Layout, Tone, and Image*

Research from successful direct-mail campaigns suggests these guidelines:

- Prefer long letters and e-mail to short ones. Contrary to conventional wisdom, the more information you give, the more likely the prospect is to act.
- Use the prospect's name and spell it correctly.
- State at least three benefits for the action you want—meeting with you, seeing a demonstration, talking with you on the phone, or buying immediately.
- Ask for a specific response or state what action you plan to take next to advance the sale.
- Offer something free for responding: a demo, research data, survey results, ten quick strategies for doing X.
- Use correct grammar. If you're careless in your grammar, how do prospects know you'll be any more careful with their order or service?
- Include complete contact information: phone, e-mail, fax, address, response form, or a link to a site to purchase.
- Make the layout easy to skim. This includes attention-grabbing headings, bulleted lists, block style, easy-to-read font, bolding and white space to highlight key items, and a postscript to reinforce the action.

TIP 446: *Never Send Out More E-mail or Letters Than You Can Follow Up On in a Week*

You don't want your prospect to remember that you didn't call to follow up as you promised. Not only does this leave a bad impression, but when you do call three weeks later, your prospect won't remember receiving your e-mail or letter. It now becomes a wasted contact. Either way, you lose.

TIP 447: *Suggest a Time Range, Not a Specific Day, for Follow Up*

A range allows you flexibility for unforeseen emergencies—sickness, travel delays, demanding clients with problems. Lack of follow-up as promised during the courtship stage of the sales cycle proves difficult to overcome.

TIP 448: *Add a "No, I'm Not Interested" Line or Box*

Consider what people are saying when they check off such a box or line on a bounce-back card or at the bottom of your direct-mail piece or e-mail. If they definitely have no interest, they'll toss the mailer away or delete the e-mail. When they take the trouble to respond to you, they're saying "I have no interest NOW" or "You haven't persuaded me to give it a try YET. But it's okay to contact me again."

So keep track of these people and stay in contact in a special way with a later offer, message, or reminder.

TIP 449: *Make Your Direct Mailings Lumpy*

Curiosity works in your favor. Add something in the envelope that relates to your product or service. A "key" to your future if you're selling outplacement services. An odd-shaped puzzle piece with the question "Are you puzzled about X?" An engraved pen to remind you of trade-show-specialty items.

TIP 450: *Use a P.S. but Don't Be Corny or "Salesy"*

Use the postscript of the e-mail or letter to remind the reader of the action and a key benefit: "If you can come into the store before May 6, we can offer another 5 percent off all upholstery fabrics." "Call me directly and I'll be happy to set an appointment over the weekend if that fits your schedule better." "Our supplier has given us an extended warranty for the next 200 customers. We hope you can take advantage of this offer."

TIP 451: *Forget the "Put It on a Page" Adage*

Length is no longer measured in words—it's measured in reading time. The number of screens or pieces of paper is less often a measure of reading time than precision, organization, and appropriateness of content.

Something well written, easy to skim, with ideas logically arranged, and that answers all questions so that buyers can act immediately, *will* motivate a buyer to act.

NETWORKING

TIP 452: *Understand the Value of Networking as a Marketing Tool*

You can't wait for all the marketing to come from the Marketing Department. After writing to stir up interest and speaking to draw a crowd, your networking skills will help you build relationships with buyers and generate trust so that they confidently give you referrals. Your personal prospecting magic is in the mix and mastery of each of these skills and strategies.

TIP 453: *Attend Trade Shows and Hang Out Some Place Other Than Your Booth*

Buyers expect to see salespeople standing in the trade-show booth and on the expo floor. They have their guard up and their resistance in place—even when stopping by your booth to ask questions. But when they sit down beside you at the table for lunch, in an educational session, or meet you at the opening gala, they see you in a different role—peer to peer.

Wear a different hat. Have questions to ask that help you relate on a different level. Interact as you would at any other business-social function in the city with the mayor, your school board president, your CPA, and your lawyer. Ask questions about them, the conference, and their business. When they reciprocate, you can explain briefly what you do. Relationships started out on this personal-social level often turn into business contacts at their own pace.

TIP 454: *Give People Their 15 Minutes of Fame*

Find a way to make your prospect a star and you may have won buyers and a whole bevy of prospects.

For example, a couple of creative organizations in the Dallas-Fort Worth (DFW) Metroplex approached *The Business Press* about jointly sponsoring a Most Influential Women recognition annually. The newspaper publicized the event, asking people to call in or write in to nominate female leaders in the Metroplex who they considered worthy of the honor. A committee of members among the newspaper staff and these two organizations selected 20 women as The Most Influential Women in the DFW Metroplex. Those who made the list had their names, biographies/accomplishments, and photographs published in the paper. The women were wined, dined, and gifted by several of the major department stores in the areas. Can you guess who the speakers were at the luncheon where these women were recognized?

The next year, same song, but with a different group of winners. The year after that, same song, third verse. Excellent marketing idea to target these influential buyers.

What group of prospects do you want to target? What kind of recognition would get their attention? Who else would want to sponsor the event with you in exchange for getting in front of these same prospects with their product or service?

TIP 455: *Serve on Committees or Boards for Charities, Foundations, or Other Nonprofits*

Why not leverage your time? You no doubt already include volunteer activities in your life—ways you give back to society. Can you combine the time you spend on those volunteer projects with responsibilities that will put you in touch with others of like mind?

TIP 456: *Join Online Chat Groups*

Obviously, you can't pitch your product or service blatantly. But you can join chat groups where you can offer genuine expertise, and invariably there will be opportunity to mention where you work and how you know what you know about products on the market and issues that are under discussion.

Then when people decide they trust you and want more in-depth information because they're in the market to buy, they can e-mail you directly.

TIP 457: *Stay in Close Contact with the Service People within Your Own Organization*

Service people are sometimes the first to know when organizations are about ready to upgrade equipment or switch suppliers. They have a network all their own. Make sure you have these people on your grapevine so you can get the word fast before competitors.

TIP 458: *Talk to Your Own Suppliers about Who's Doing What*

Your own suppliers serve you and probably your competitors. If you ask the right people the right questions, you get the news first: Who's unhappy with whom? Who's downsizing? Who's paying on time and who's not? Who's in legal hot water? Who has money to spend? Who has a new model coming up? Your suppliers may not be connecting the dots, but you can. The faster you connect the dots, the faster you can knock on the doors of the right prospects at the opportune time.

TIP 459: *Join Networking Clubs*

Networking clubs organize around one key objective—for their members to show up, exchange business cards, and profit from their liaisons with each other. Generally, you align yourself with others who are in a complementary business, selling noncompeting products or services to the same prospects.

For example, if a prospect needs an architect to design a new home, they'll probably need a banker to finance a mortgage, a real estate agent to sell their current home, a moving company to move their family, and maybe a landscape company and a pool company. If you were in a networking club, you might organize a lead-sharing group to trade leads among representatives from salespeople offering these services and products.

TIP 460: *Make Sure Your Friends and Family Know What You Offer and How You Can Help*

No one wants to be a pest to their family and friends and bring up business at every family get-together. But neither should you take it for granted that Uncle Levy knows that you're a CPA in business for yourself and in need of new clients. How would your second cousin LeJune know that you work for a software consulting business, specializing in warehouse and inventory solutions?

Speak up and let people know what you do.

TIP 461: *Remember Names As If Future Business Depended on It*

Listen when introduced. Pay attention rather than trying to think of something clever to say in response. If you don't understand the name, ask the person to repeat it. During the course of the conversation, repeat it a couple of times. Make a mental association with the name. When you get a business card, make a note on the back of the card about the person's appearance, interests, and your connection so you remember that individual.

TIP 462: *Send Follow-Up Notes without Any Pitch or Reference to What You Do*

If you think the person might be a prospect or otherwise might be a good connection for you, follow up after the networking contact. Instead of a pitch in your note, e-mail, or letter, simply reference the conversation you had, mentioning that you enjoyed chatting. Follow up with anything you promised such as an article or phone number of a colleague or a Web site of interest.

TIP 463: *Love 'Em, Leave 'Em, Link 'Em*

After you make connections, build on the relationship in small ways. Even if they aren't in a position to do business with you, you never know when they'll be able to send business your way. As you change jobs and even areas of the country, provide them with your new contact information and let them know what new responsibilities you have. Become known as their link to interesting and significant people.

When you leave an account—move, get assigned, change jobs—say goodbye, just as you would with friends and family. Life's too short not to turn your business colleagues into friends. E-mail makes it easy to stay in touch; writing makes the effort memorable, because it sets you apart.

Finally, link them to your replacement with a nice introduction in the same message so your organization can hold on to the account during this dangerous transition period.

TIP 464: *Use Preprinted Stationery with Your Contact Information and Your Positioning Slogan*

Obviously, you want your contacts to remember what you do—that's the point of business networking. To accomplish your purpose without having to mention that directly in your e-mail or letter, let your stationery (or signature block in e-mail) do the trick.

For example, my own stationery carries our training company's slogan: "Increasing Productivity through Effective Communication." That slogan appears on our business cards, letterhead, postcards, brochures, Web sites, signature blocks, and product packaging.

TIP 465: *Attend Social Functions with a "PR Buddy"*

At networking functions, it's generally a "no-no" to talk business too often or too long. But no one says your colleague can't toot your horn for you. Plan to attend such functions with a colleague from another organization.

During the evening, take the opportunity to mix and mingle and mention each other as the occasion arises.

Example: "Oh, have you met Paul Sarasota over there? He's with XYZ Corporation. He helps organizations like yours develop their plans to do. . . ." He'd be a good person for you to talk to about Y. Let's walk over there, and I'll introduce you."

Example: Said to new acquaintances who just mentioned new tax legislation and their plans to take their business public: "While you're here, you should meet Emily Smyra, with Smyra and Smith, Inc. They have an accounting firm that specializes in handling businesses like yours. She's done some incredible work in tax law and IPOs."

TIP 466: *Let People Know You Appreciate Referrals*

People do what they get rewarded for doing. When you receive a referral, make it an occasion. Send a gift certificate for two to dinner at a favorite restaurant, a good biography, a fruit basket, or take them to lunch.

TIP 467: *Help People Give You Ripe Referrals*

Sometimes people fail to give referrals not because they don't have confidence in your product or service, but because they can't think of who might be able to use your products or services. You have to help them.

Mention what you do specifically and profile your typical buyer for them. Example: "As you might guess, referrals are really important to me. I'd appreciate your letting me know of someone who could use my services. If you have colleagues at other hospitals who might be looking for rebuilt equipment of this nature—those going through major cutbacks particularly, or small clinics that do their own testing—those are my primary clients. Do you have a couple of colleagues who might be looking for such rebuilt machines?"

Such an inquiry tells them exactly what kind of prospect fits your profile. Specific requests lead to specific referrals—those ripe for your offerings.

TIP 468: *Follow Up Referrals with the Speed of Light*

Never wait more than a couple of days to contact the referral. Can you remember what you wore the day before yesterday? Can you remember what you had for dinner last Thursday? Do you remember the last time you talked to a family member—outside your immediate household—and what they said they planned to do over the weekend?

If the referred person calls the source before they call you, and the source can't remember the context of your discussion and the specifics and benefits of your offering, all advantage has been lost. Your credibility has cratered.

9

SELLING AT THE POINT OF SERVICE

With better-educated buyers in a competitive culture, sales has become everyone's job. The organization with the most employees on the "look out" for sales opportunities wins—wins the customer, wins the profit, wins the right to stay in business.

But then "selling" is not a new idea. Couples sell each other on saying "I do." Coaches have to "sell" a team on drill, skill, and the thrill of a win. Actors sell an audience on the authenticity of the characters they play. Doctors sell their credibility to diagnose and then their recommended treatment. Lawyers sell their theories and evidence. Politicians sell their philosophies. Engineers must sell their calculations, theories, and designs to the team and executive management.

Both personal selling and professional selling is a way of life for almost everyone in today's organizations.

This chapter will focus on those in a customer service role who can up-sell, cross-sell, open leads, or actually close transactional sales during a customer service interaction.

TIP 469: *Assume You're the Lone Ranger*

Many buyers have already shopped on the Internet before they call, and they expect whoever answers the phone to guide them through their many choices. They expect everyone who works for an organization to be knowledgeable about its products and services—or at least as knowledgeable as they are after having searched the Internet, your Web site, and the competitors' products and services.

You'll also have other customers who may not know you can help them with problems unless you recognize their need and begin the dialogue. They never ask; they never buy.

In either case, impatient callers and visitors are no longer willing to wait while you find someone else with the answers and techniques to lead them through the plethora of choices. Everybody wants something, and they want it now.

You may be the first stop—and the last—on the way to the competitor's door.

TIP 470: *Understand Why Customers Automatically Say "Thanks, but No Thanks"*

Other variations of this line include: "I'm busy," "I'm not interested," "I don't need it," or "I'll check it out on the Internet and call you back."

Such comments follow years of habitual responses generated from inappropriate opening lines. You're probably aware of your own experiences in shopping when someone has asked, "May I help you?" and you've automatically responded, "No, I'm just looking." Later you ask for their help—and buy something.

Customers think that a positive response, such as "Yes, I'm interested," will either commit them to buy or commit them to time-consuming conversation unrelated to their mission. Neither should be true.

TIP 471: *Never "Pump" Customers; Engage Them*

Opening lines chart your conversation course. In any sales conversation, stay away from closed questions—those that can be answered with a brief word or phrase. They tend to halt the sales process in its tracks. Example:

"Are you looking for any particular color?"

"No, not really."

"Did you have a particular style in mind?"

"Not particularly."

"Are you familiar with our layout here?"

"Yes, I am."

"Well, if I can help you, please let me know."

"Okay."

End of conversation. To engage buyers, you have several choices: You can refer to a previous positive sales or service experience to put buyers at ease and let them know you value and remember their business; you can ask how they like a previous product or how your current service is working out for them; or you can find something you have in common to start the conversation on a warm, friendly note. For example, if they comment that they're about to leave on vacation, by all means ask where they're planning to travel and wish them a nice trip.

Generally, the best conversation starter is to ask them about their use or plans for your product or service. For example, if you're selling software, you might ask: "How familiar are you with this application?" That should open the conversation so that you can understand where and how you can help them make a buying decision. If you're in a service role, you'll probably engage them in conversation about the goals or projects they have planned.

If you do it well, how you initiate and guide the conversation will be seamless to the customer.

TIP 472: *"Dust" Information from Customer to Customer*

In a customer service role, you will undoubtedly hear many new uses, tips, precautions, and nice-to-know tidbits of information about your products or services. In fact, software manufacturers often organize user groups for the very purpose of facilitating customer information sharing.

Take the initiative in passing on such ideas from one buyer to the next in a more informal way as you come into contact with your customers to complete their paperwork, renew their accounts, process their payments, install their equipment, deliver their services, or troubleshoot problems. Of course, you may want to protect confidentiality on sensitive issues without including names, but mentioning additional uses for your offerings creates a heavier use and bigger demand.

TIP 473: *Gather Valuable "Renewal" Information without Sounding like the Local DA*

When customers call to report a change of address for billing purposes or to ask about prices, you certainly don't want to prolong the call so that it becomes an onerous task to deal with you. As you engage customers in conversation, it's often easy to ask one or two additional questions, the answers of which you can add to your database or pass along to your sales team.

Examples: If you service life insurance accounts, you might ask when the customer's property or auto insurance renews. If you work for a bank and open personal checking accounts, you might ask if they'll need to move their small business account also. If you sell cable service, you might ask when their long-distance carrier contract on their cell phone renews and pass on that information to your cellular phone division.

Don't barrage customers with a litany of questions. Parcel them out, one or two per encounter, until you have your customer profiled and can turn over leads to the appropriate departments for follow-up.

TIP 474: *Replace "Anything Else?" with Specific Suggestions*

Great idea; weak phrasing. When you walk up to the checkout register and the clerk asks, "Anything else?" what's your typical response? "Nope. That's it." Why? If you could think of anything else on your own, you would have selected it or asked about it, right? At this point, you need prompters.

When your customers buy a product or service, suggest something specific—something that other customers typically buy with that same product or service. (See the following tips for ideas.)

TIP 475: *Suggest Better Items, Models, Services, or Values*

Up-sell your customers when possible. Your buyers will remember and appreciate quality and value long after the memory of initial cost has faded.

TIP 476: *Suggest Larger Orders or Quantities, Extended Subscriptions, or Better Guarantees*

Generally, the bigger the up-front commitment by the buyer, the greater the value. For example, if you decide to improve your health by changing your diet, you can buy one week's worth of fruits and vegetables. If you go back to the old habits after a week, you probably will not have done much to improve your health. But if you commit to buy three months' worth of fruits and vegetables, you're much more likely to form lasting eating habits.

The same holds true with almost any product or service arrangement: As you encourage your buyers to join in lockstep with you for a longer period of time, you have a greater opportunity to influence their business operations or their personal lifestyle for the long term.

TIP 477: *Suggest Related Items, Accessories, and Services*

Examples: "Do you need socks with these shoes?" "Did you save room for our famous pecan pie?" "This brooch would really make a great accent piece for this jacket, wouldn't it?" "I suppose you'll also want the carrying case to protect it, right?" "Of course, we can train all your employees on this new system once we have it installed." "Will you want to book a rental car when you get to L.A.?" "We also offer consulting services to help you with additional projects that can come up from time to time as you run into tax implications when operating in different states."

All of these are examples of up-selling related services, products, and accessories. Suggestions succeed in letting your customers know what's available and reminding them of ways you can help them.

TIP 478: *Suggest Custom Rather Than Generic*

To paraphrase Frank Sinatra, the marketplace is filled with customers willing to pay a premium for suppliers who'll let them "have it my way." When your company can customize, tell customers about it.

TIP 479: *Suggest Convenience*

Remind customers to buy from you other things that they typically buy elsewhere but may not know you have available.

TIP 480: *Dig Customers out of Their Ruts*

Innovation keeps organizations alive. Your current customers are often the last to know about your organization's newest products or services. Buyers start buying one product or service line from you and forever pigeonhole you only in that niche.

Every few years we do a comprehensive survey of our clients and provide them with a complete list of our current training programs. We then ask them to check those they were not aware of before the survey. We're always amazed at the result. Those that originally bought business or technical writing from us think we only do writing programs. Those that originally bought sales presentations think we only do sales presentations. Those that bought a negotiations course remember only that we do negotiations. Ditto for proposal writing and running effective meetings or listening programs. Yet, we know they have received direct mailings, e-mail, books, press releases, newsletters, and articles to the contrary.

Informing clients typically takes a personal phone call to get their attention—and retention—at least until the news has passed their eyes the proverbial six times. That's where you as a customer service agent come in. You may be in touch with an account more often than the actual assigned sales professional. Continually look for opportunities to tell customers about services, products, and options they currently are not buying from your organization.

TIP 481: *Look for Ways to Say Yes Instead of No*

"We don't do that." "We don't have any." "We're out of stock." "That's not our division." These are all too common phrases, and they sound like "So there. Don't call us. Stay away and don't come back—ever!" They send buyers to the competition much faster and more often than necessary. Instead, offer other options.

TIP 482: *Watch Out for Malpractice*

If you don't know, say so. A few years ago, the bank in my Dallas-Fort Worth suburb advertised their automated time and temperature line. Customers dialed the number and an automated voice came on and said, "This is X Bank. Time, 11 AM. Temperature, 54 degrees." One day when I had difficulty getting through on the line, I phoned the operator and asked her to check the line. After a moment, she returned to the line and said, "I'm sorry, but there's some problem and I can't get through either. I'll report it. But I have the time myself. It's 1:26. And the temperature is, oh, about, . . . I'd say it feels about 30, maybe 35 degrees. I was just out for lunch, and I definitely needed my jacket."

She gets an A for a service attitude and she gave me my chuckle for the day. But definitely, I knew I wasn't getting a meteorologist's view. As a service agent, if asked a technical question outside your area of expertise, say so rather than risk giving an inaccurate answer and losing a sale. You always can tell buyers what you know for certain, and then put them in touch with the appropriate person for a more complete sales dialogue.

TIP 483: *Never Question "Why?" When a Buyer Asks a Favor*

Paying customers expect service. Sometimes your willingness to go the extra mile marks the only difference between you and your competitor. Expectations run in two categories: high and higher.

TIP 484: *Educate Your Buyers without Making Them Feel like Bozos*

A big part of selling involves receptivity, and receptivity reflects interpersonal skills. As you service your customers and explain to them why their widget won't work, avoid a patronizing and impatient tone.

Nobody wants to feel stupid—even if the widget won't work because it's not plugged in.

TIP 485: *Leave Editorial Comments Unspoken*

How often have you stood in line at the airline counter, the grocery store, or department store and overheard someone talking about the last customer they'd serviced? "What a jerk! He touched every package in here—and I had just straightened the whole counter." "Did you hear that moron—he couldn't make up his mind if his life depended on it." "Her elevator doesn't go all the way to the top—I bet she wakes up in a new world every morning."

When customers hear you disparage another customer in their presence, they'll assume you have the same attitude about them. With that in mind, they'll not likely be an eager buyer in the future.

TIP 486: *When Buyers Have Had a Bad Experience, Use a "Triple A" Play*

Acknowledge. Assess. Accelerate. *Acknowledge* a past problem. *Assess* why that situation or condition existed, and explain why that condition is no longer a problem. Then *accelerate* the discussion to the current situation—how things stand today and what the buyer can expect from your products or services currently.

TIP 487: *Differentiate between Statements, Questions, and Objections*

Consider the following customer comments:

- "I thought maintenance was included in the $399 price."

- "Does everybody have to complete this three-page form before they get service?"
- "Is my account supposed to be handled out of your Chicago office or here?"

Are these statements, questions, or objections? Ask different service agents and you'd probably get different opinions, depending on voice inflection, tone, content, and body language. All of those clues give meaning to the actual words.

When talking to your customer in a sales or service situation, don't jump to conclusions. First, verify by probing for meaning. Then accept a statement, answer a question, or address a concern or objection.

TIP 488: *Use the Side-by-Side Technique to Resolve a Problem and Rebuild Rapport*

Positioning yourself eyeball to eyeball while discussing a negative situation sets up a confrontational atmosphere that undercuts a selling opportunity. Customers want you to see things from their viewpoint when you're servicing their account or investigating their needs. To increase rapport, move physically so that you can stand shoulder to shoulder with a customer (looking in the same direction) to convey subtly that you are seeing things from their point of view as you discuss problems.

TIP 489: *"Own" a Lead Until You've Transferred the Baton*

When you hand off a lead to colleagues in another department, unfortunately, they may be operating under a peak workload, off the job sick, or out of the country on a family emergency. You hope they've planned for such emergencies and have back-up assistance. But when that's not the case, your customer referral shouldn't fall through the cracks.

To prevent that from happening, you can do several things:

- State a range for the call-back rather than a specific day or time.
- Give the customer the appropriate person or department and contact information so that if the colleague doesn't call back in a timely fashion, the caller can initiate another inquiry.
- Use your own tickler file and check back with the customer in a few hours or days (whichever is appropriate for your business) to verify that someone from the other department has contacted them.
- Escalate the referral to the next higher level in the organization if no one has followed up with the customer after a reasonable time.

Own the lead and stake a claim for your organization. Don't let buyers have to go to the competition for help with their problems.

TIP 490: *Follow Up and Keep Your Promises*

The sales team gets a paycheck to *bring in* customers. Service agents get a paycheck to *keep* customers. Your service often means the difference between a one-time sale and a repeat, long-term client.

Research studies conducted by various organizations report that customers stop doing business with organizations based on a single incident of poor customer service. What's worse, they tell their friends and colleagues—on average nine to ten other people—about that poor service and this also colors other people's opinions and buying habits.

One of the strongest things you can do to create additional sales opportunities for your organization is to provide exceptional service with a friendly, positive attitude—all the time, on time. Do what you say you will.

After the sale happens, you *are* the organization.

10

MOTIVATING YOURSELF

TIP 491: *Turn Feedback into Mini Growth Seminars*

When you receive negative feedback from either a buyer or your management team, the temptation from mediocre performers is to become defensive. Star performers will seek out others and ask for advice—their sales manager, peers, even other trusted clients with whom they've built a friendship: "How would you suggest I handle a similar situation next time?"

TIP 492: *Make Difficult Customers a Personal Challenge*

Sometimes the only difference between feeling pumped or deflated is your long-term view. Determine to make difficult customers a personal challenge.

If that seems to be impossible or even repugnant to you, calculate the amount of your annual income that comes from that difficult customer's account. Then divide that dollar amount by the average number of hours you must spend dealing with that person. Finally, ask yourself, if it is worth $X per hour to deal with this person. If it is, instead of focusing on the headache the customer causes, remind yourself of how much you're earning for the time spent dealing with this individual.

TIP 493: *Keep a Journal to Share at Sales Meetings*

As you work, keep a list of questions, ideas, what-ifs, and success and failure stories to share with colleagues. Average performers will sit around and complain about meaningless sales meetings that eat up their selling time. Star performers, on the other hand, can make weekly or monthly sales meetings meet their needs—even if they have to manipulate the agenda.

If you have a difficult buyer, ask for suggestions. If you have an implementation issue in a complex sale among multiple buyers, put the scenario on the table for discussion among your colleagues. If you're looking for the perfect case history to include in your proposal, ask colleagues to rack their brains for applicable past projects.

Compiling a running list of these matters as they surface keeps your meetings meaningful and, over time, marks you as the go-to person with all the answers.

TIP 494: *Evaluate Significant Sales Calls*

Many star performers focus so heavily on self-improvement that they sometimes forget to study their wins. Isolate any new principle, technique, question, or tidbit of data that helps you close a deal. What tipped the sale in your favor? Was it thorough needs analysis? Technical knowl-

edge? Persistence? Getting to the right person? Astute handling of political enemies within the buyer organization? Timing? Phrasing of the implications of the benefits you could deliver? Credibility builders?

Record these personal success techniques and categorize them by
product or service line for periodic review. Everybody needs refreshers.

TIP 495: *Keep an "ATTA-BOY" or "YOU GO, GIRL" File*

Record positive comments you receive from satisfied clients, along
with any e-mails or letters sent to you or forwarded to you from your
management about how you've handled an account. When handling a
tough buyer situation or after losing a sale, pull out this file and psych
yourself up to move on to new opportunities.

TIP 496: *Create Your Own Motivational Quotes Log*

Start a log of your own collection of customer comments about your
work. You can use these as a motivational computer screen saver, or you
can pull your favorite sayings and quotes (with attribution, of course)
from published sources to use as screen savers, to frame for your wall, or
to create a personal calendar with daily pop-ups.

BOOKS: Selected Titles

Speak with Confidence: Powerful Presentations That Inform, Inspire, and Persuade

E-Writing: 21st Century Tools for Effective Communication

Your Signature Life™: Doing Your Best in All Things

Communicate with Confidence: How to Say It Right the First Time and Every Time

Good Grief, Good Grammar

To the Letter: A Handbook of Model Letters for the Busy Executive

Great Personal Letters for Busy People

The Complete Letterwriter's Almanac

Clean Up Your Act: Effective Ways to Organize Paperwork and Get It out of Your Life

Executive's Portfolio of Model Speeches for All Occasions

The New Secretary: How to Handle People As Well As You Handle Paper

Send Me a Memo: A Handbook of Model Memos

Writing for Technical Professionals

Winning Sales Letters

Get a Life without Sacrificing Your Career

Ten Smart Moves for Women

Get Ahead, Stay Ahead

The Worth of a Woman's Words

Well Connected: Power Your Own Soul by Plugging into Others

Mother's Gifts to Me

The Esther Effect

Little Book of Big Questions: Answers to Life's Perplexing Questions
Love Notes: From My Heart to Yours
Fresh-Cut Flowers for a Friend
First Thing Monday Morning

VIDEOS

Writing for Results
Writing in Sensitive Situations
Thinking on Your Feet: What to Say During Q&A
Basic Steps for Better Business Writing (series)
Business Writing: Quick, Clear, Concise
Closing the Gap: Gender Communication Skills
Cutting Paperwork: Management Strategies

CUTTING PAPERWORK: Support Staff Strategies Audios

People Power
Write to the Point: Business Communications from Memos to Meetings

SOFTWARE

Selling Skills and Strategies: Create and Deliver Sales Presentations with Impact
Selling Skills and Strategies: Everyone Sells: Selling Skills for the Non-Salesperson
Selling Skills and Strategies: Manage Your Pipeline, Accounts, Time
Selling Skills and Strategies: Negotiate So That Everyone Wins
Selling Skills and Strategies: Thinking on Your Feet: Handling 11 Difficult Question Types
Selling Skills and Strategies: Write Proposals That Win the Business
Selling Skills and Strategies: Write to Your Buyers: E-mail, Letters, Reports

Effective Writing

Effective Editing

Good Grief, Good Grammar

More Good Grief, Good Grammar

Ready, Set, NeGOtiate

2001 Model Business Letters

2001 Sales and Marketing Letters

8005 Model Quotes, Speeches, & Toasts

Model Personal Letters That Work

WORKSHOPS

Email Excellence™

Effective Writing

Technical Writing

Developing Winning Proposals

Good Grief, Good Grammar

eService Communications

Customer Service Communications

Presentations That Work® (oral presentations)

Communicate with Confidence®

Listening Until You Really Hear

Resolving Conflict without Punching Someone Out

Leading and Participating in Productive Meetings

Negotiating So That Everyone Feels like a Winner

Increasing Your Personal Productivity

Managing Information Overload

SPEECHES

Communicate with Confidence®

From the Information Age to the Communication Age: The 10 Cs

The Gender Communication Gap: "Did You Hear What I Think I Said?"

Communicating CARE to Customers

Write This Way to Success

Platform Tips for the Presenter: Thinking on Your Feet

Get a Life without Sacrificing Your Career

You Are Your Future: Putting Together the Puzzle of Personal Excellence

The Plan and the Purpose—Despite the Pain and the Pace

The Worth of a Woman's Words

Ten Smart Moves for Women

Q

Dianna Booher, CSP, CPAE, is an internationally recognized business communication expert and the author of 41 books, numerous videos and audios, and an entire suite of Web-based e-learning products to improve communication, sales effectiveness, and productivity. She is the founder and president of Booher Consultants, based in the Dallas-Fort Worth Metroplex. Her firm provides keynotes and communication training (written, oral, interpersonal, gender, customer service, and sales) to some of the largest Fortune 500 companies and government agencies such as IBM, ExxonMobil, Kraft Foods, Caterpillar, PepsiCo, Frito-Lay, Nokia, JC Penney, Merrill Lynch, Morgan Stanley, Lockheed Martin, Ernst & Young, GlaxoSmithKline, Texas Instruments, Scientific Atlanta, MD Anderson Cancer Center, Verizon, and the Army & Air Force Exchange Service, to name just a few. *Successful Meetings* magazine recently recognized her in their list of "21 Top Speakers for the 21st Century."

Dianna Booher and her team travel internationally presenting programs on sales and communication and delivering motivational keynotes on life balance and personal productivity. For more information about booking Dianna or her staff, please contact:

Booher Consultants, Inc.

2051 Hughes Road

Grapevine, TX 76051

Phone: 817-318-6000

mailroom@booher.com

<www.booher.com>

Share the message!

Bulk discounts
Discounts start at only 10 copies. Save up to 55% off retail price.

Custom publishing
Private label a cover with your organization's name and logo. Or, tailor information to your needs with a custom pamphlet that highlights specific chapters.

Ancillaries
Workshop outlines, videos, and other products are available on select titles.

Dynamic speakers
Engaging authors are available to share their expertise and insight at your event.

**Call Dearborn Trade Special Sales at 1-800-245-BOOK (2665)
or e-mail trade@dearborn.com**

Dearborn™
Trade Publishing
A **Kaplan Professional** Company